Asbury
Publishing

# Thoughts Are Things®

Roz —

Everything begins

as a THOUGHT.

David Meine

# Thoughts Are Things®

*Daily readings for children and their families*

By David Moon

www.davidmoon.com

Edited by William S. Rukeyser
Illustrations and design by Bora Shehu and Jona Shehu

There aren't many original ideas in life.
Please forgive any overlooked recognitions.
Those errors are unintentional and they are mine.

Wheeler David Moon, III
Knoxville, Tennessee
www.davidmoon.com

*Thoughts Are Things*® is available for multi-copy
purchase discounts. For information, contact
books@davidmoon.com.

ISBN 978-0615869520

Printed in the United States of America

Asbury Publishing
www.asburypublishing.com

*A child who is not deservedly confident in himself will become an adult who longs to be someone else.*

*~ David Moon*

# Gratitude

If not for the confidence and teaching of John Majors I would likely have never known what was possible and what it takes to prepare for it. Coach, thank you for showing me the ocean and how to get there.

Thanks to Bill Rukeyser for his decades of support in so many ways. George Doebler, Jim Sanders, Armistead Smith and Patrick Carr are the best spiritual mentors a man could have.

The wonderful and witty illustrations of Bora Shehu and Jona Shehu bring these ideas to life.

Without Micah Herren this book would have never happened. Without Micah a lot of good things would never happen.

Finally, I want to thank my children, Bethany and Wheeler, for inspiring this book and my wife, Sien, for inspiring me.

# Introduction

If, as Warren Buffett tells us, the chains of habit really are too light to be felt until they are too heavy to be broken, then the perfect age to begin a daily discipline of reflection is as young as possible. All humans, but especially children, are susceptible to the impact of repetitive teaching and suggestion. The best time to introduce a program of positive life skills is long before a child's daily exposure to the dampening effect of worldly pessimism.

The lessons in *Thoughts Are Things* are simple. Certain themes are repeated throughout the year, each in a unique way to appeal to a young, beginning reader.

Each day the youngster is offered three distinct items: a concept for the day, a reading that expounds on that day's concept and a repetitive affirmation that your child will quickly memorize and is encouraged to recite aloud after completing that day's reading throughout the year:

*I am smart, happy and healthy. My parents love me. God has given me many gifts. I can do anything I want to if I make a plan, concentrate and work toward it every day.*

All of the theology in these 365 days emanates from those four simple sentences. Gratitude. Responsibility. The power of the mind. The importance of God. The need for action. Positive thinking. Unconditional love.

When my children were in the third grade, I began writing these daily thoughts for them as a way to share my philosophy of life. Admittedly, this philosophy isn't original, as it combines Judeo-Christian doctrine with that of Greek thinkers, American Indian spiritualists and modern-day inspirers. It even includes the influence of a football coach or two.

Although they are written for school-age children, these daily readings became the impetus for great family discussions about God, personal responsibility, planning, love, gratitude, work and relationships.

My hope for you is that these readings will inspire your children to seek wisdom, as they learn who they are and work to become those people.


Peace.

David Moon

# January 1st
## New Year's Day

It is important to have dreams.

# Dream big.

You really can have anything you want in life if you make a plan, concentrate and *work toward it every day*. Most people just dream about what they want. Very few people actually make a plan. Even fewer really work toward their dreams.

What are your dreams? What are you going to do *today?*

I am smart, happy and healthy. My parents love me. God has given me many gifts. I can do anything I want to if I make a plan, concentrate and work toward it every day.

# Look forward;

that's where the future is.

Don't spend time worrying about
things that have already happened.
You can't change the past.

You can live today. You can plan
for tomorrow. You can set goals,
make plans and work toward
the things you want. Focus your
mind on what you want.

Don't waste any of your mind
being upset about—or even
celebrating—things in the past.

I am smart, happy and healthy. My parents
love me. God has given me many gifts. I can do
anything I want to if I make a plan, concentrate
and work toward it every day.

## *January 3rd*

Birthday of Millard Fuller
Founder of Habitat for Humanity
1935

# Thank God

for what you *do* have;
don't complain about what you *don't* have.

Did you break your arm? Be thankful;
some kids don't have arms.

Did you lose a toy or favorite shirt?
Did you get in a fight with a parent?
Some children live in an orphanage,
with few toys, and don't have parents.

Some kids don't even have a home. They
live with friends, in a homeless shelter or
maybe even sleep outside or in a car.

When something bad happens,
be thankful; it might have been worse.

I am smart, happy and healthy. My parents
love me. God has given me many gifts. I can do
anything I want to if I make a plan, concentrate
and work toward it every day.

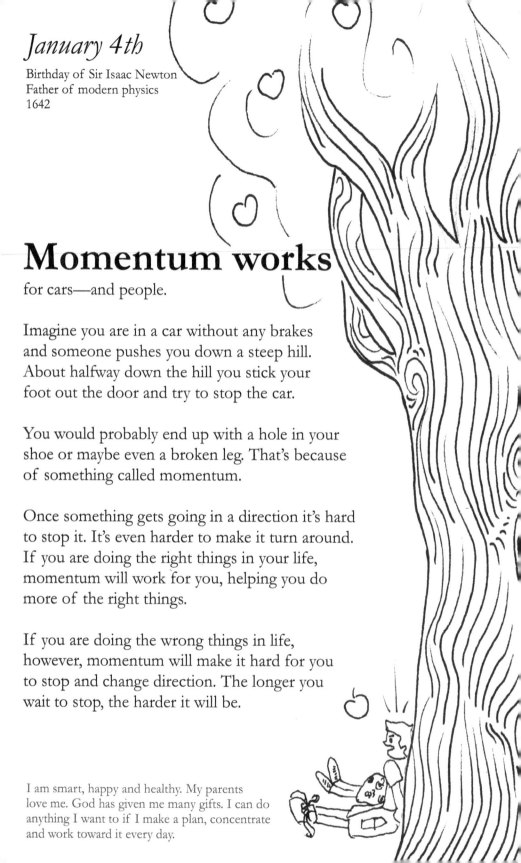

## January 4th

Birthday of Sir Isaac Newton
Father of modern physics
1642

# Momentum works

for cars—and people.

Imagine you are in a car without any brakes
and someone pushes you down a steep hill.
About halfway down the hill you stick your
foot out the door and try to stop the car.

You would probably end up with a hole in your
shoe or maybe even a broken leg. That's because
of something called momentum.

Once something gets going in a direction it's hard
to stop it. It's even harder to make it turn around.
If you are doing the right things in your life,
momentum will work for you, helping you do
more of the right things.

If you are doing the wrong things in life,
however, momentum will make it hard for you
to stop and change direction. The longer you
wait to stop, the harder it will be.

I am smart, happy and healthy. My parents
love me. God has given me many gifts. I can do
anything I want to if I make a plan, concentrate
and work toward it every day.

It doesn't matter if you

# think you can

do something or if you think you can't.
You are probably right whichever one you believe.

Our minds have an incredible power to take
the things that we believe and help us turn
those beliefs into actual, physical things.

Be careful what you believe. Your mind is
going to believe whatever you tell it,
even if it is silly or isn't true.

You can do anything.
You have great talents and gifts.

I am smart, happy and healthy. My parents
love me. God has given me many gifts. I can do
anything I want to if I make a plan, concentrate
and work toward it every day.

# You already know what's right and wrong.

Many times in our lives we can't decide what to do so we look at the actions of the people around us. When we do that, we are letting them make our decisions. We lose control of our own decisions and, in some cases, our soul.

In most situations, you never need to ask anyone what is right or wrong. God has given each of us a compass inside ourselves that tells us the direction that is right. We only need to look at the compass.

I am smart, happy and healthy. My parents love me. God has given me many gifts. I can do anything I want to if I make a plan, concentrate and work toward it every day.

# Everyone has the same number of hours each day.

Do you ever wonder how some people seem to do more than others each day? How can that be?

Everyone has 24 hours each day. That equals 1,440 minutes, or 86,400 seconds. That's it. That's what everyone gets whether you are 5 years old, 15 years old, or 50 years old.

The only difference is what each of us chooses to do with our 86,400 seconds. If you wish you were getting more things done, don't complain about it. Look at how you spend your time. Are you spending your time on the things that are most important to you?

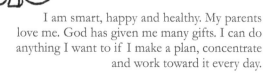

I am smart, happy and healthy. My parents love me. God has given me many gifts. I can do anything I want to if I make a plan, concentrate and work toward it every day.

# Your mind has super powers.

The mind is the most powerful part of your body.
You can do more with your mind than you can with
your arms or legs. Your mind is the control system of
all your other muscles.

When you use your mind and think about something,
there is a mystical power that brings you and that thing
closer together. Be sure that you always use your mind
to think about good things, so you will move
closer to good things. You do not want to
move closer to bad things.

I am smart, happy and healthy. My parents
love me. God has given me many gifts. I can do
anything I want to if I make a plan, concentrate
and work toward it every day.

# Things often look different to the other person.

When you are in an argument or disagree with someone, you almost always think that you are right. You wish that the other person would just see things as you see them.

Maybe they don't understand what happened earlier, or they don't know what problems you have. If they understood those things, they might act a little differently toward you. They might be nicer.

Now look at it from the other person's point of view. They feel the same way. They are having the same thoughts.

When someone else is in a bad mood or you disagree with them about something, try to see it from their point of view.

I am smart, happy and healthy. My parents love me. God has given me many gifts. I can do anything I want to if I make a plan, concentrate and work toward it every day.

# Make something better today.

Wherever you go, you should want it to be better because you were there. Will you do something to help someone today? Will you do something to make yourself better today?

These can be little things. Help your mother, brother or sister with something without being asked. Do something for a classmate or teacher. Give something to someone who needs it.

Make yourself better. Practice your penmanship. Read something extra. Exercise. Play a new game. Work on your math.

Be better and help others to be better, too.

I am smart, happy and healthy. My parents love me. God has given me many gifts. I can do anything I want to if I make a plan, concentrate and work toward it every day.

# Time is more valuable than money.

Without time, you wouldn't be able to enjoy
anything else. How do you spend your time?
If you look at how you spend your time,
you will see what is most
important to you.

Don't waste time. Once you spend an hour
doing something, you will never get
those 60 minutes of your life back.
Make sure that you spend your time
doing important things. Be with your friends
and family, work toward your goals and
make yourself better.

I am smart, happy and healthy. My parents
love me. God has given me many gifts. I can do
anything I want to if I make a plan, concentrate
and work toward it every day.

# A plan

is a lot more than a list
of dreams and hopes.

It is important to have dreams and goals.
Think about the things you want
to do in life.

What do you want to accomplish?
Think about those things every day.

But you must do more than dream. You
must take action. The first step in taking
action is making a plan. After you decide
what you want, you have to decide what
you are going to do to get it.

You may think that some people are
simply lucky and get everything they want.
The people who make the best plans and
work the hardest in life always seem to be
the luckiest.

They make their own luck.
It starts with a thought,
then a plan. Then action.

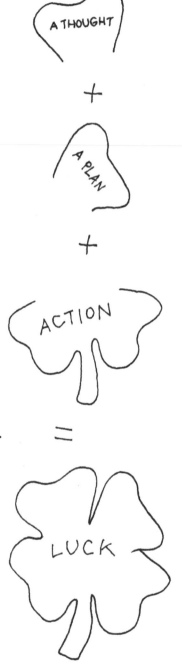

I am smart, happy and healthy. My parents
love me. God has given me many gifts. I can do
anything I want to if I make a plan, concentrate
and work toward it every day.

# Set goals.

Decide what is important to you.

You are never too young to have a goal. The younger you are, the more powerful your goals will be. If you set goals today, you have a longer time to work on them and you will be able to do more great things in your life.

If you will set one or two major goals right now, you will be doing something most adults never do. You will probably also achieve things that most adults never achieve.

I am smart, happy and healthy. My parents love me. God has given me many gifts. I can do anything I want to if I make a plan, concentrate and work toward it every day.

*January 14th*

Bad things happen to everyone.

# How you react is what is important.

When something makes you mad, it has already happened to you, and once something has already happened, you can't change it. But you can control how you react to it. In fact, how you react is about the only thing you can control.

Successful people don't cry if things don't go their way.
They don't kick the ground. They try again.
They try harder. They stay focused on their goal.

Your success in life will depend on what you do when things don't go the way you want them to.

LETS PLAY A GAME
WHILE WE WAIT

I am smart, happy and healthy. My parents love me. God has given me many gifts. I can do anything I want to if I make a plan, concentrate and work toward it every day.

# You can't smile on the outside and frown on the inside.

It is impossible for your mind and body to disagree with each other. One will always control the other. If you feel bad but begin to act happy, soon you will feel that way.

I am smart, happy and healthy. My parents love me. God has given me many gifts. I can do anything I want to if I make a plan, concentrate and work toward it every day.

If you avoid work, then good things will probably
avoid you. The best things usually come to those who

# go and get them.

Watch someone fishing from a boat. What does he do?
He gets a pole, some fishing line, a hook and some bait.
He puts the bait in the water, tries to attract a fish,
then pulls the fish into the boat.

He does not simply float down the river and hope
that fish jump into his boat.

A good fisherman works hard at catching fish.
A fisherman who does not work at it very much
does not catch very many fish.

I am smart, happy and healthy. My parents
love me. God has given me many gifts. I can do
anything I want to if I make a plan, concentrate
and work toward it every day.

# We attract

what we think and talk about.

There is a power in life that brings
things together that want to be together. It's like a
magnet of life. If you think about bad things all day
long, bad things will follow you around.

The mind is a magnet that can be programmed to
attract either positive or negative things.

If you always think and talk about good things,
you will be amazed at the good things that happen.
Happy people will want to be around you.

If you think about bad things, only bad
people will want to be around you.

WE'RE HERE!

I am smart, happy and healthy. My parents
love me. God has given me many gifts. I can do
anything I want to if I make a plan, concentrate
and work toward it every day.

# Always do more

than you say you will.

If you tell someone you are going to pick up
three bags of trash, pick up four. If you are
going to surprise your parents, surprise them by
doing more than they expect you to do. It is
much better to do more than people expect
you to do than to do less.

I am smart, happy and healthy. My parents
love me. God has given me many gifts. I can do
anything I want to if I make a plan, concentrate
and work toward it every day.

# Don't tip-toe into the cold water.

There are times in your life when you have to do things that aren't fun. They are really hard.

Don't wait to do those things.
Don't try to do a little at a time.

Just do it. Do it all at once. Jump in the water.

You will get it done faster and you will feel so much better when you are finished.

I am smart, happy and healthy. My parents love me. God has given me many gifts. I can do anything I want to if I make a plan, concentrate and work toward it every day.

*January 20th*

It is impossible to hide the truth forever.

# Always tell the truth,

even if you think it doesn't matter.

It always matters. You will be developing a good habit.

People will learn to trust you. If people trust you and you always tell the truth, you will never have to pay the consequences of being caught in a lie.

If you tell a lie, the truth will eventually always come out.

I am smart, happy and healthy. My parents love me. God has given me many gifts. I can do anything I want to if I make a plan, concentrate and work toward it every day.

# Plan

for the future;

# don't worry

about it.

Most people worry about things that never happen or things they can't control. We worry that it might rain. We worry about something someone might say to us. We worry about what other people might think about us.

Don't worry about these types of things. You can't do anything about them.

Instead, plan for the future. Where do you want to go and what do you have to do to get there? Plan for the things you can control. Work on those things today, but don't worry about those things today.

How can you tell the difference between working and worrying? When you work toward a goal, it makes you feel better. When you worry about it, it makes you feel worse.

I am smart, happy and healthy. My parents love me. God has given me many gifts. I can do anything I want to if I make a plan, concentrate and work toward it every day.

# Every day should be Thanksgiving Day.

No, you don't need to eat a bunch of turkey and dressing every day. But you don't need to wait until November to give thanks for your blessings.

The more you thank God and others for the gifts they give you, the more blessings you will continue to receive.

One great habit to start is a Gratitude Journal. Every day, write something in your journal for which you are grateful.

I am smart, happy and healthy. My parents love me. God has given me many gifts. I can do anything I want to if I make a plan, concentrate and work toward it every day.

# If you always do what is right,

the right thing will happen more often.

Sometimes it just takes a little while.

Sometimes you will tell your parents,
teacher or friend something and they may
not believe you. Do not be discouraged.

Just keep telling the truth about everything.

Eventually the other person will realize
that you are the kind of person who
always tells the truth—and they will believe you.

This only works if you always tell the truth.

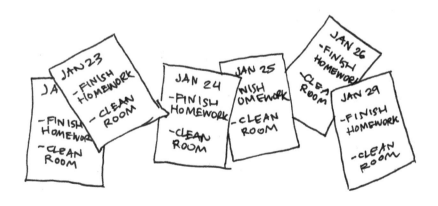

I am smart, happy and healthy. My parents
love me. God has given me many gifts. I can do
anything I want to if I make a plan, concentrate
and work toward it every day.

# Impress yourself,

not other people.

Don't do things or wear clothes just because that's
what everyone else is doing. That's called peer pressure.
When you know what you want to do, do it.
It doesn't matter what other people think.

Parents make this mistake sometimes, too.
They will buy a car or house, or maybe they
will take a job, because they think it will impress someone.

Do what you think will make you happy, not other people.

BEST SCULPTURE EVER!

I am smart, happy and healthy. My parents
love me. God has given me many gifts. I can do
anything I want to if I make a plan, concentrate
and work toward it every day.

# **Fear**

is something that is in your mind.

Who controls your mind? You do.

No matter how hard you try, there will be times in your life that you are afraid of something. That's okay; it happens to everyone.

Most of the things we fear in our lives, however, never happen. Maybe you're afraid a small green man will be in your underwear drawer or that someone will put hot sauce in your toothpaste tube.

Guess what? Go look in your drawer and bathroom. No little green man. No hot sauce.

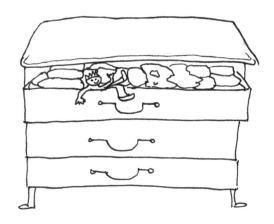

I am smart, happy and healthy. My parents love me. God has given me many gifts. I can do anything I want to if I make a plan, concentrate and work toward it every day.

# First impressions are important.

Most people will make up their minds about you within the first minute or two after meeting you. They will decide if they think you are smart or well educated. If you are trying to get a job, someone might make a decision about hiring you within a couple of minutes.

This is why it is important to always be on your best behavior when you meet someone new. Shake adults' hands. Look them in the eye. Speak in a strong tone. Use proper language.

You are developing habits today that you will have the rest of your life.

I am smart, happy and healthy. My parents love me. God has given me many gifts. I can do anything I want to if I make a plan, concentrate and work toward it every day.

# Do something nice

for someone today—someone who doesn't ask for it.

It's nice to help someone who needs it. If your parent or teacher is trying to carry a television set and can't do it alone, you can help. Together you can get something done that neither one of you could do alone.

Another great thing to do is surprise people with something nice that they could do for themselves. Surprise your dad with a glass of cold water after he mows the yard. Shock your sister by making her bed one day. Talk to a kindergarten student at school.

These are easy, nice things that you can do that will surprise the other person and help both of you have a good day.

THANK YOU, YOUNG MAN

I am smart, happy and healthy. My parents love me. God has given me many gifts. I can do anything I want to if I make a plan, concentrate and work toward it every day.

*January 28th*

# God is everywhere,

even if it isn't always obvious.

God came to Moses in a burning bush.
Sometimes he sent angels to deliver messages.

We don't see many burning bushes or angels flying
around anymore. But that doesn't mean we don't
see or hear God.

When we are in nature, among the trees, mountains,
rivers and animals—God is there. God shows himself
through other people: our friends, family and
neighbors. All of these things are connected in
some mysterious way.

If God is in those things, then God is everywhere,
including in you.

I am smart, happy and healthy. My parents
love me. God has given me many gifts. I can do
anything I want to if I make a plan, concentrate
and work toward it every day.

If you can't

# be trusted
# in the little things,

people won't you trust you in the big things.

Always tell the truth.
If you say you are going to do something,
ALWAYS do it. This is called being *trustworthy*.

Like many things in life, being trustworthy is a habit.

Trusting someone else is a habit, too.
If someone lies to you, even if the lies aren't
about important things, you can't know
if they are telling the truth about things
that are really important.

I am smart, happy and healthy. My parents
love me. God has given me many gifts. I can do
anything I want to if I make a plan, concentrate
and work toward it every day.

If you're going to get your rear
end kicked, you ought to at least

# learn something

from it.

Sometimes things happen to us that are so bad
that it feels like we've been beaten up in a fight.
Maybe it's something at school, like a test or an
argument with a friend. Maybe it's something at home.

When bad things happen, there is always a lesson
to be learned. Maybe the lesson is what not to do.
Maybe you can learn what you should have done.

If you don't learn the lesson, however, it's like
you have been beaten up for nothing.

I am smart, happy and healthy. My parents
love me. God has given me many gifts. I can do
anything I want to if I make a plan, concentrate
and work toward it every day.

When things are hard, **you are getting stronger.**

If you exercise hard, you will become tired. Your muscles will get sore and you will get very sweaty. But your muscles, heart and lungs get stronger when you work them hard.

Your life is the same way. If something happens that you don't like or you have to try many times to get something done, you are getting stronger. When things don't go your way, don't get upset. Hardships create strength.

I am smart, happy and healthy. My parents love me. God has given me many gifts. I can do anything I want to if I make a plan, concentrate and work toward it every day.

*February 1st*

# Everyone needs to know they are loved.

There are many different types of love.
Love for a friend. Love for a brother or sister.
Love for a parent. Love for a stranger in need.
Love for a husband or wife.

It's hard to define love, but some people say that
"God is love." That's nice. It means that any
time you love someone God is there. You are
showing a little of God to that person.

We know that everyone needs God. If God
is love, that means everyone needs love.

Think about how you feel when
someone tells you that they love you.
Everyone needs to hear that.

I am smart, happy and healthy. My parents
love me. God has given me many gifts. I can do
anything I want to if I make a plan, concentrate
and work toward it every day.

# Have courage to try new things.

You might really like scrambled eggs and bacon, but imagine if you had to eat that for every meal the rest of your life. Yuck!

When you try something new, you are taking a chance. You might try something and not like it. You might take a chance and fail. That's fine.

If you never fail, you aren't trying enough new things. If you never try anything new, you will never experience anything new. You will just keep having the same experiences over and over.

Boring!

I am smart, happy and healthy. My parents love me. God has given me many gifts. I can do anything I want to if I make a plan, concentrate and work toward it every day.

## *February 3rd*

Sometimes the best thing you can

# **say** is
# **nothing.**

When someone says something that is wrong, you
don't have to disagree with them; sometimes it is okay
just to be quiet and not start an argument.

Sometimes two people might be sitting on the front porch
reading or just thinking about life. Maybe you and your father
or mother are watching the sunset. There is nothing wrong
with sitting quietly, listening to nature, God or maybe even
your own silent voice.

Conversation is great. When two people talk about something
that is important to one of them, that is a wonderful thing.

Sometimes, however, it is also wonderful to
sit and listen to the quiet.

I am smart, happy and healthy. My parents
love me. God has given me many gifts. I can do
anything I want to if I make a plan, concentrate
and work toward it every day.

# God speaks

to those who take the time to listen.

One of the ways we talk to God is to pray.
We give thanks and sometimes we ask for help.

If we want to hear the answers to our prayers,
we have to listen. We need to sit quietly and think
about the people and things that are important to us.
Close your eyes and think about your "thankfuls."

In the quiet time while you are doing this,
what comes to your mind?

I am smart, happy and healthy. My parents
love me. God has given me many gifts. I can do
anything I want to if I make a plan, concentrate
and work toward it every day.

# February 5th

Birthday of Garrett Morgan
Inventor of the traffic signal
1877

If you don't know where you are going,

# how will you get there?

What if you had a week to go on vacation, so you got in your car and left, but you had no plan? You just decided to drive until you got there. How would you know when you were there? When you came to a traffic signal, how would you know which way to turn?

You wouldn't. You need a plan.

Life is the same way.

Always have plans for what you want to do or you will be like a person driving a car without any idea of where he is going.

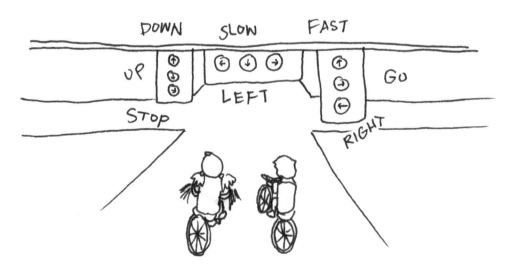

I am smart, happy and healthy. My parents love me. God has given me many gifts. I can do anything I want to if I make a plan, concentrate and work toward it every day.

There is only one safe way to

# brag: with your actions.

Do you know anyone who is really good at something?
A good student or musician? Maybe a good teacher?

How do you know they are good? You watch them.

The person doesn't have to brag or tell you
they are good for you to know it.

So why do people brag?

Because they are concerned about what
other people think about them.

If you are really worried about what other
people think, don't tell them how good
you are, just be quiet and show them.

I am smart, happy and healthy. My parents
love me. God has given me many gifts. I can do
anything I want to if I make a plan, concentrate
and work toward it every day.

In most things,

# there is plenty for everybody.

Too often we think that if someone else gets something, we can't have it. We become jealous.

If your brother gets a certain toy, maybe you get mad because you wanted that toy.
Or maybe one of your parents seems to be showing your sister more attention than you. That might make you feel bad.

But your parents have more attention. They have more love to give. Don't get upset.

Remember that the more of something you give, the more you will probably get.

I am smart, happy and healthy. My parents love me. God has given me many gifts. I can do anything I want to if I make a plan, concentrate and work toward it every day.

Good baseball players

# don't swing at every pitch.

To accomplish great things in life, you must show courage.

That is, you must be willing to be brave and take chances. You must also know when not to take a risk, because some risks are not worth taking. Wise adults learn what kinds of risks are worth taking—and which ones aren't. They compare risks and rewards.

I am smart, happy and healthy. My parents love me. God has given me many gifts. I can do anything I want to if I make a plan, concentrate and work toward it every day.

# You are more valuable

than any fancy car, big house or any amount of money.

No matter how upset you get about things,
remember that you are a child of God, created in
the image of God. Your brain is more powerful
than any computer. You have the ability to think,
feel, love and solve problems—something that no
other animal or machine can do.

You are valuable. Take care of yourself as you'd
take care of a fancy piece of jewelry or a million
dollars, because you are worth so much more than that.

I am smart, happy and healthy. My parents
love me. God has given me many gifts. I can do
anything I want to if I make a plan, concentrate
and work toward it every day.

If you can't **control yourself,**

you probably won't control much of anything.

Do you ever feel you do things and you don't understand why? Maybe you don't want to be disrespectful, or maybe you want to make your bed every day. But for some reason, you just can't seem to do what you want to do.

Begin to control your habits today. It's hard to control yourself, and it gets harder as you get older.

If you can't control yourself in the easier things, you almost certainly won't be able to with the harder things.

I am smart, happy and healthy. My parents love me. God has given me many gifts. I can do anything I want to if I make a plan, concentrate and work toward it every day.

# No one can do everything on their first try.

Thomas Edison invented the electric light bulb.
He said he failed 10,000 times before he finally got it right.

If you are trying to do hard things or really great things,
you will have to try many times before you get it right.

Great golfers start at a young age and practice hours each day.
Guess where most of their shots go when they first start playing?
Into the woods, sand and water.

It takes time and practice to be good.

When you were an infant, you would try to stand...then you would
fall down. Over and over again. Stand up. Fall down. Stand, fall.

Finally, you stood and stayed up. All of life works that way.

I am smart, happy and healthy. My parents
love me. God has given me many gifts. I can do
anything I want to if I make a plan, concentrate
and work toward it every day.

Don't be jealous or angry at the
person who has something you want.

# Go and earn
# it for yourself.

You can't make yourself better by hurting someone else.
There is nothing wrong with wanting things as long as those
things don't become more important to you than people.

If you try to take the things you want from
other people instead of earning them yourself,
you obviously love things more than you do people.

I am smart, happy and healthy. My parents
love me. God has given me many gifts. I can do
anything I want to if I make a plan, concentrate
and work toward it every day.

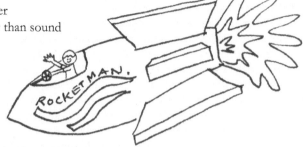

# How high is "up?"

That's how powerful your mind is.
Imagine if you got in a rocket ship that was
pointed straight in the air and you took off and
flew in a straight line. If you never ran out of
oxygen, how far could you go?

A very, very, very, very long way.
Maybe forever. No one really knows,
because no one has ever been that far.

Your mind is the same way. No one knows
how far it can go. You can do more with
your mind than you think you can.

The only limits on the power of your mind are
the ones you put on it. Your brain and
imagination are like that rocket ship in outer
space. They can go much farther than you think.
First you have to get your mind to "blast off"
and then never stop flying.

I am smart, happy and healthy. My parents
love me. God has given me many gifts. I can do
anything I want to if I make a plan, concentrate
and work toward it every day.

# Love can't be earned.

It is a gift.

There is nothing your parents or a friend can do to make you love them. You either love someone or you don't. You may get mad at someone from time to time, but that doesn't mean that you don't love them.

Sometimes the people who love you will become mad or disappointed in something you do, too. This doesn't mean that you have lost their love. Since you can't do anything to earn someone's love, you can't make someone stop loving you, either.

I am smart, happy and healthy. My parents love me. God has given me many gifts. I can do anything I want to if I make a plan, concentrate and work toward it every day.

# Don't waste time.

One of the major differences between people who do great things in life and those who just "get by," is that the people who do great things realize that they only get 24 hours a day—and each one of them is important.

Both groups of people get the same number of hours each day, but the ones who just "get by" waste many of them doing nothing productive: watching TV, working on things or projects that don't really matter—or maybe doing nothing at all.

The people who do great things in life know that once a day in their life is gone, they can never get it back.

I am smart, happy and healthy. My parents love me. God has given me many gifts. I can do anything I want to if I make a plan, concentrate and work toward it every day.

# Choose friends who make you better.

One of the biggest influences in your life will be your friends. If you spend your time with people who behave and make good grades, you probably will too. And if your friends get into trouble, there is a real good chance you will get into trouble.

Be proud of your friends.
If you were a boss, would you hire that person?
Would they work hard and make you proud?
Those are the kind of people who should be your friends.

If you want to be wise, be around wise people.

OUR FRIENDS ARE THE BEST!

I am smart, happy and healthy. My parents love me. God has given me many gifts. I can do anything I want to if I make a plan, concentrate and work toward it every day.

## February 17th

Birthday of Henry Steinway
Founder of the Steinway Piano Company
1797

When you are afraid of
something, don't run from it.

# Stand up to it.

At times in everyone's life they are afraid of something.
But most of the things we fear never happen.

Have you ever been bitten by a snake or had a
piano fall on your head?

Probably not.

If you're afraid of something, ask yourself why. Don't try to hide
from your fear. Try to be logical and figure out if the thing you are
afraid of is likely going to happen.

Like a piano falling on your head,
it probably won'

I GOT IT

NO, I GOT IT!

I am smart, happy and healthy. My
parents love me. God has given me
many gifts. I can do anything I want
to if I make a plan, concentrate
and work toward it every day.

# Make a plan.

Everybody wants good things to happen to them. They hope. They pray. They ask others.

Then they hope some more.

That's not a plan.

When you make a plan, you are in charge. You don't have to hope. You don't have to wish for good luck. You will know exactly how your plan works.

Don't wait and hope good things happen. Go get them yourself.

I am smart, happy and healthy. My parents love me. God has given me many gifts. I can do anything I want to if I make a plan, concentrate and work toward it every day.

## February 19th

Birthday of Nicolaus Copernicus
German astronomer
1543

# Never be afraid to stand alone.

It's easy to do what everyone else is doing,
but that does not make it right.
Sometimes the crowd is wrong.

Some of the greatest inventors and thinkers
in the world were laughed at by their friends.

For thousands of years, people thought that
the earth was the center of the universe and
that the sun and planets revolved around us.
The few people who believed that the sun
was the center of the universe were laughed
at. Some were sentenced to prison for their
beliefs even though they were right.

I am smart, happy and healthy. My parents
love me. God has given me many gifts. I can do
anything I want to if I make a plan, concentrate
and work toward it every day.

# Someone looks up to you.

Is there someone in your life whom you admire? Maybe a parent, teacher or priest. Maybe it's one of your parents' friends. You probably watch the things they do, the way they talk and other things they do. Even if you don't realize it, those people influence the way you act.

Believe it or not, there is someone who looks at you the same way.

Maybe it's someone at school. It could be a younger cousin or the brother or sister of a friend of yours. But there is a young person watching the things you do and listening to the things you say–and wanting to act like you.

Be a good example to that person.

I am smart, happy and healthy. My parents love me. God has given me many gifts. I can do anything I want to if I make a plan, concentrate and work toward it every day.

# Problems look a lot bigger from the front side.

When things are hard and you are struggling with a problem, it can seem like you might not ever be able to get over it or have a way to deal with it.

You will.

When you look back at your problems, sometimes they just don't look as big as they did when they were happening.

It's like a mountain that looks huge until after you climb it.

I am smart, happy and healthy. My parents love me. God has given me many gifts. I can do anything I want to if I make a plan, concentrate and work toward it every day.

# Good things

don't happen by accident.

If you want something good or great to happen, someone has to take action. You can't just talk about it.

Imagine if George Washington had just talked about America being free from England. He could have sat around and told people that one day he was going to fight for America's freedom.

Or he could have just stayed home and hoped that someone else became "the father of our country."

What if everyone did that?

There would be no America. There would be no great things, because nothing great happens when people sit around just talking and waiting.

I am smart, happy and healthy. My parents love me. God has given me many gifts. I can do anything I want to if I make a plan, concentrate and work toward it every day.

# If you have to do something, do it.

Don't wait. Take action. If there is something to be done, don't hope that if you wait a day or two that you might not have to do it.

If you have a project at school, do it now. Don't start the day before it is due. Study early so you will have plenty of time.

If you take care of your responsibilities as soon as possible, you will have more time in case something goes wrong.
And if nothing goes wrong, you will be able to enjoy yourself better, because you won't be worrying about what you have to do.

I am smart, happy and healthy. My parents love me. God has given me many gifts. I can do anything I want to if I make a plan, concentrate and work toward it every day.

# Think about what you want,

not what you don't want.

Deep inside your mind there is
a computer that is always working
whether you realize it or not. Even
when you are asleep this deep part
of your mind is busy working on the
things that you put in your mind.

If you give a problem to this
computer, it will work to help
you solve it.

But this part of your mind—the
part that is always working—doesn't
know if you want something or not.
It doesn't know right from wrong.
It just goes to work on whatever
you put in there.

If you want to quit being mean to
your dog (or sister or brother), don't
tell yourself that you want to quit
being mean. Tell your mind that you
want to "be nice."

I am smart, happy and healthy.
My parents love me. God has
given me many gifts. I can do
anything I want to if I make a
plan, concentrate and work
toward it every day.

## February 25th

No matter how hard you try,

# bad things are going to happen sometimes.

Some days won't be as good as others.
When that happens, you have a choice.

Will you get upset and spend all of your energy
worrying about the days that don't go just the
way you want them to?

Or will you let your mind focus on the great things
that do happen in your life? Doing this will
obviously put you in a better mood.

When you decide what you are going to think
about, you also decide your own mood.

I am smart, happy and healthy. My parents
love me. God has given me many gifts. I can do
anything I want to if I make a plan, concentrate
and work toward it every day.

# You must have confidence

that you can succeed in your goals—or you won't.

The messages we send our mind are very powerful.
They decide whether our minds work for us or against us.

When our mind believes that something is going to happen,
that thing is more likely to happen.

I am smart, happy and healthy. My parents
love me. God has given me many gifts. I can
do anything I want to if I make a plan,
concentrate and work toward it every day.

What you are doing today is
because of something

# from your past.

Look around you. Everything in your
life is there because of decisions that
someone made in the past. The things
that you, your parents, friends and
teachers have done have brought you
to where you are in life today. It has not
been an accident.

Where will you be seven years from
now? What about 10 or 20 years from
now? Wherever it is, it will be because
of the decisions and actions you are
making now.

I am smart, happy and healthy. My parents
love me. God has given me many gifts. I can do
anything I want to if I make a plan, concentrate
and work toward it every day.

# Keep your life in balance.

In school, do you spend the entire year studying math? All day, each day, do you do nothing but arithmetic?

Of course not. You study several subjects so you will become a well-rounded, well-educated person. By the time you graduate from high school, you will know something about a lot of different subjects.

It is good to have a major goal in life, but there are different parts of your life that need attention. You need to take care of your body. You must take care of your mind. You need to have good relationships with friends and family. You need to maintain your relationship with God.

Keep these parts of your life in balance.

I am smart, happy and healthy. My parents love me. God has given me many gifts. I can do anything I want to if I make a plan, concentrate and work toward it every day.

# February 29th

(If this is a leap year!)

If a frog had wings, he wouldn't
hit his belly every time he leaped.

# Everyone has certain skills.

We also have certain limitations. If you are
seven feet tall and weigh 300 pounds, you
probably aren't going to be a very good
horse jockey. There is no sense in telling
yourself, "But if I were just two feet
shorter I could be a good horse jockey."

You aren't two feet shorter.
You aren't going to be two feet
shorter. Get over it.

Don't look for excuses about why
you can't do things. Don't get
upset about things that are
impossible for you to have.

Concentrate on
the things that you do
have or the things
you can change.
Frogs don't have wings.
Neither do you.

I am smart, happy and healthy. My parents
love me. God has given me many gifts. I can do
anything I want to if I make a plan, concentrate
and work toward it every day.

# You don't drown if you fall into deep water.

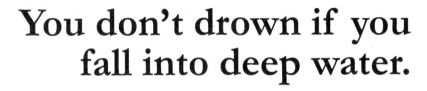

You drown if you just lie there.
Your success in life depends on how you react
when something bad happens. Will you do nothing,
like a person just lying in the water, waiting to drown?

Or will you refuse to die? Will you work and do
whatever it takes to make the situation better?
Will you fight to get up?

Hoping things get better won't help.
You have to *do something*.

I am smart, happy and healthy. My parents
love me. God has given me many gifts. I can do
anything I want to if I make a plan, concentrate
and work toward it every day.

# March 2nd

Birthday of Theodore Seuss Geisel (Dr. Seuss)
American writer and cartoonist
1904

# Be the best *You* that *You* can be.

You are different from everyone who has ever lived before. Your body, your brain, your spirit, your strengths—everything about you has come together to make a person who is special and unlike anyone else.

Do not try to be anyone else. Enjoy being you.

Sometimes in life we think we should act like other people. We might try to look like them or talk like them. Maybe they are doing something and we think that means we should do it, too.

You should only do something if it makes sense for you. If you try to be someone else, you are wasting a wonderful gift that God gave you.

I am smart, happy and healthy. My parents love me. God has given me many gifts. I can do anything I want to if I make a plan, concentrate and work toward it every day.

# Your friends influence your beliefs.

Everything you are around has some kind of influence on you. The weather, cars, animals, people...yes, people. Especially people.

Do you think people are usually good or bad? Do you believe God is full of love? Or do you believe God is mean? Do you believe you can do anything you want to do? Or do you believe luck is more important?

These are all important beliefs. Whoever you listen to and whoever you make your friend will have a strong influence on what you believe about everything when you become an adult.

Be sure that the people you are around believe the kinds of things you want to believe.

I am smart, happy and healthy. My parents love me. God has given me many gifts. I can do anything I want to if I make a plan, concentrate and work toward it every day.

# Always be early.

Always. Absolutely always.

When you are early to see someone, you are saying that person is important to you. If you have a project at school and you finish a few days or weeks early, that project must be important to you.

When you are early, it shows that you are serious and have respect. If you are late, it shows disrespect and that you aren't serious.

I am smart, happy and healthy. My parents love me. God has given me many gifts. I can do anything I want to if I make a plan, concentrate and work toward it every day.

If you do something wrong to someone,

# apologize

as soon as possible.

No matter how hard we try, we all do things we wish we hadn't. Maybe we say something that hurts someone's feelings. Maybe we even get mad and break something. There are all sorts of things we might do to hurt someone. Sometimes the other person might not even know about it.

You must apologize when you make a mistake.

If you've done something that can be fixed, you must fix it.

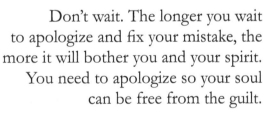

Don't wait. The longer you wait to apologize and fix your mistake, the more it will bother you and your spirit. You need to apologize so your soul can be free from the guilt.

I am smart, happy and healthy. My parents love me. God has given me many gifts. I can do anything I want to if I make a plan, concentrate and work toward it every day.

# Only you control your own mind.

There are lots of things in your life at your age that you don't get to control. Where you live. What you eat. Where you go to school. When you go to bed.

As you get older you get to decide more of these things.

None of these are as important as controlling your mind. The great news is that you get to control your mind from the time you are born. No one ever controls that for you.

You are the only person who can put you in a bad or good mood. You get to decide whether to think about positive things or negative things. You can waste your mind on silly things or use it to create great relationships and do great things. You can make your own plans, dreams and goals.

I am smart, happy and healthy. My parents love me. God has given me many gifts. I can do anything I want to if I make a plan, concentrate and work toward it every day.

Don't let other people

# be in charge of your happiness.

People do things that upset us. Sometimes our parents do things that make us angry. A brother or sister certainly can. People often do things that we wish they wouldn't.

Try not to let what other people do make you happy or sad. If other people can make you angry, you are giving them one of the greatest powers in the world: the power over your happiness.

The only person you should let control your happiness is you.

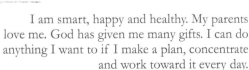

I am smart, happy and healthy. My parents love me. God has given me many gifts. I can do anything I want to if I make a plan, concentrate and work toward it every day.

# Develop a plan.

It is important to have dreams. Think about
the things you want to do in life. What do
you want to accomplish? Think about
those things every day.

But there is more. You must take action.
The first step in taking action is making a
plan. After you decide what you want, you
have to decide what you are going to do.

There must be a "to do" part for a dream
to have a chance of becoming reality.

I am smart, happy and healthy. My parents
love me. God has given me many gifts. I can do
anything I want to if I make a plan, concentrate
and work toward it every day.

# Think before you speak.

There are many things in life that you can undo.
If you tie your shoelaces into a knot, you can undo
the knot. If you build a sand castle and don't like it,
you can knock it down and start over.

Once you say something, however, you can never
take it back. When words leave your mouth,
the message becomes permanent.

Think about what you want to say before you say it.

Some people feel uncomfortable with silence.
They talk and babble about nothing so there is always
some noise. When they do this, they
usually don't think about what they are saying.

If someone doesn't think about what they are
about to say, they are more likely to
say something stupid.

I am smart, happy and healthy. My parents
love me. God has given me many gifts. I can do
anything I want to if I make a plan, concentrate
and work toward it every day.

## *March 10th*

When we become too busy, there are some answers
in life we cannot find. Sometimes when we need
the answer to a problem, we simply need to

# stop, think
# and listen.

Hearing the voice of God is the same way.

When our minds and hearts are busy—even if they
are busy with important things—it is hard for us to
hear the small voice that brings big wisdom.

I am smart, happy and healthy. My parents love me.
God has given me many gifts. I can do anything
I want to if I make a plan, concentrate and work
toward it every day.

# You are responsible for your own actions. Never blame others.

If you are disappointed in something, don't blame someone else for your problem. A lot of times that's the first thing we want to do. We don't want to admit that maybe we made a mistake.

Sometimes bad things happen even though nobody made a mistake. We still want to blame somebody.

If you have a problem in your life, you have to fix it—even if someone else caused it. You are responsible for you. Don't waste your energy trying to blame someone else for the problems in your life; just go and fix them.

I PROBABLY SHOULDN'T HAVE USED BETHANY'S TEDDY BEAR AS A FOOTBALL

I am smart, happy and healthy. My parents love me. God has given me many gifts. I can do anything I want to if I make a plan, concentrate and work toward it every day.

# March 12th

The more you think about something,
the more you become like it.

This might not make sense when you first
read about it. "If I think about monkeys,
will I become a monkey?" No, but if all you
think about is monkeys, you won't become
much of anything, because you will waste all
of your time thinking about monkeys!

Your mind will take you closer to the things
you think about, even if you don't want it to.

There is a power that brings you closer to
whatever you think about. Be sure to

# think about the things you want.

I am smart, happy and healthy. My parents
love me. God has given me many gifts. I can do
anything I want to if I make a plan, concentrate
and work toward it every day.

Always ask for more work.

# Do more than you are asked to do.

The people who have the most are the people who do the most. It doesn't matter if you are talking about the most fun, the most money, the most business or the most happiness.

So if you want more, you need to do more.

Do more than you are asked to do. Do more than your parents ask. Do more than your responsibilities. Keep doing this as you get older. If you want more money at work, do more than your boss expects you to do.

I am smart, happy and healthy. My parents love me. God has given me many gifts. I can do anything I want to if I make a plan, concentrate and work toward it every day.

# Time
is the most valuable
natural resource in your life.

There are many things that a person
might waste in his life. Food, water,
paper...all sorts of things.

If you waste time, however, you can never
get it back. No one can give you more time.
You can't save time and use it later.

Time is the one resource that you can't
replace if you waste it. Treat it like a
precious resource—because it is.

I am smart, happy and healthy. My parents
love me. God has given me many gifts. I can do
anything I want to if I make a plan, concentrate
and work toward it every day.

# Believe.

The Bible says that a man can do or have anything he wants if he believes he can. When you have a thought, your mind sends that thought to your entire body and to everyone and everything around you. Every muscle, bone and fiber in your body receives the signal and begins working on that thought.

When you believe something strongly enough, it is like having a force field around you that protects you from failure and only allows in success.

Believe. If you believe you can do something, you'll be right. If you believe you can't do it, you'll be right, too.

I am smart, happy and healthy. My parents love me. God has given me many gifts. I can do anything I want to if I make a plan, concentrate and work toward it every day.

# March 16th

When you

# help another person,

you are also helping yourself.

When we see someone in need, we often feel that
we ought to help them because they need us.

That is true. But there is also a bigger need. When
we help someone we are also helping ourselves be a
better person. This keeps us from being selfish.
It helps the other people around us.

It makes the whole world a better place.

I am smart, happy and healthy. My parents
love me. God has given me many gifts. I can do
anything I want to if I make a plan, concentrate
and work toward it every day.

# Good luck is not going to come looking for you.

You have to let it know where you are.

It's nice if good things happen when we don't think we've done much to make them happen. We call it good luck.

However, good luck doesn't happen by accident. We don't just stumble into it. We prepare ourselves to receive good luck.

Everyone has this opportunity.

We make plans. We work hard. We do the right things. These are the ways that we let good luck know that we are ready.

Then when an opportunity comes our way, we take advantage of it.

It takes a lot of work to be lucky.

COME OUT COME OUT WHEREVER YOU ARE!

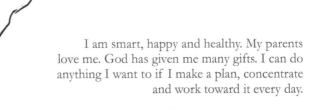

I am smart, happy and healthy. My parents love me. God has given me many gifts. I can do anything I want to if I make a plan, concentrate and work toward it every day.

# Take care of your body;

it's the only one you have.

If your body is tired or sick, it will be hard for you to
work on your goals or do anything fun. You won't
enjoy being around other people and no one will
enjoy being around you.

When you are sick, the only thing that matters
is trying to get well.

Believe it or not, you can influence how much
you are sick. You can decide to be well and healthy.
If you treat your body well, it will treat you well.

Eat the right foods. Exercise. Treat your body like it is
something that has to last your whole life—because it does.

I am smart, happy and healthy. My parents
love me. God has given me many gifts. I can do
anything I want to if I make a plan, concentrate
and work toward it every day.

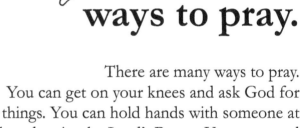

# Try different ways to pray.

There are many ways to pray.
You can get on your knees and ask God for
things. You can hold hands with someone at
church and recite the Lord's Prayer. You can stand
on a mountain top and listen for the wisdom
that God provides in quiet moments.

You can practice any of these types of prayer—at
almost any time—by creating your own quiet time.

The important thing is that you create a habit of
connecting with a Higher Power every day.
This is hard. It is difficult not to let your mind
stray. That's okay; it happens to everyone.
Like everything, the more you do it the
better you will be at it.

I am smart, happy and healthy. My parents
love me. God has given me many gifts. I can do
anything I want to if I make a plan, concentrate
and work toward it every day.

# Your mind is like a garden.

If you plant a seed in your garden, water the seed and take care of it, a mighty tree can grow.

When we think about something, we are putting an idea into God's Garden: our mind. Any thought we put in there will grow if we take care of it.

How do you take care of a thought? Concentrate on the thought several times each day. Spend a minute in the morning asking God to help you take care of your thought.

Make plans. Set a goal.

Then do something every day that helps the thought grow. Before you know it, you will discover the power of God's Garden.

I am smart, happy and healthy. My parents love me. God has given me many gifts. I can do anything I want to if I make a plan, concentrate and work toward it every day.

Knowledge is one thing that can
never be taken away from you.

You will collect many things during your life.
The best things to collect are in your mind.
Things like knowledge.

If you know something or know how to do
something, no one can take that away from you.
The more you know, the more you can
control your own future.

# Collect knowledge, not stuff.

I am smart, happy and healthy. My parents
love me. God has given me many gifts. I can do
anything I want to if I make a plan, concentrate
and work toward it every day.

*March 22nd*

# Don't be worried

when you are afraid.

If you ever find yourself afraid of something, you are normal. Everyone is afraid at some point in their life.

Some fears are logical. Some fears don't make any sense at all. It doesn't matter; if you are afraid, you are afraid.

The question is this: when you are afraid, what are you going to do? Will you be worried about the terrible things you think might happen? Or will you try to concentrate on the things that you can control and try to ignore the things you can't control?

Everyone has fears. What will you do with yours?

I am smart, happy and healthy. My parents love me. God has given me many gifts. I can do anything I want to if I make a plan, concentrate and work toward it every day.

# You must learn to walk before you run.

Imagine a little baby who is just barely able to hold her head up. She is lying on the floor, rolling around, making little baby noises.

All of a sudden, she stands up, runs across the room, jumps over the couch, turns a cartwheel and sprints out of the room!

Probably not.

There are some things that you have to do to get ready for other, harder things.

Everything we do in life gets us ready for whatever we are going to do next.

Don't be upset if there are things you want to do but aren't able to do yet. You can't jump over the couch until you learn to stand up.

I am smart, happy and healthy. My parents love me. God has given me many gifts. I can do anything I want to if I make a plan, concentrate and work toward it every day.

# March 24th

When something is hard,

# God is preparing you

for something better.

Some people in life face great challenges. Other people face very few challenges at all. The people who achieve the most and are the happiest are the ones who learn to deal with difficult challenges.

Every time we face something hard and overcome it, it makes us stronger. When he presents us with difficult times, God is preparing us for even greater things in the future.

I am smart, happy and healthy. My parents love me. God has given me many gifts. I can do anything I want to if I make a plan, concentrate and work toward it every day.

If you have to catch two cats, chase

# one at a time.

Have you ever watched a cat run around inside a house or in a yard? Cats are quick. Try sometime to catch one that doesn't want to be caught.

It is hard.

Now try to chase them both at the same time. It can't be done.

Concentrate on one cat—and catch that cat. Then you can turn your attention to the second cat.

When you start something, finish it. Then you can worry about "trying to catch the second cat."

I am smart, happy and healthy. My parents love me. God has given me many gifts. I can do anything I want to if I make a plan, concentrate and work toward it every day.

# Character

is what you do when
no one is watching.

It's easy to do the right thing when a parent or
teacher is standing right next to you watching you.
You will get in trouble if you don't.

What do you do when there is no one around?
That is who you really are.

One day your parents and teachers will be gone.
The only person standing there will be you.

What will you do?

Start making good decisions now and you
will do the right things when you are older.

I am smart, happy and healthy. My parents
love me. God has given me many gifts. I can do
anything I want to if I make a plan, concentrate
and work toward it every day.

Success requires good habits.

# You must be *consistent.*

Some people have a hard time working on the same thing very long. They might practice basketball ten minutes, then decide to watch television. After a few minutes, they might do some of their responsibilities, like cleaning their room. While cleaning their room, they might get distracted by a barking dog and go outside and play with a pet.

This is no way to become a very good basketball player.

The people who become good at things are able to concentrate on them for long periods of time. They not only concentrate for many minutes (or sometimes hours) each day, but they are able to concentrate over a period of days, weeks or even years.

I am smart, happy and healthy. My parents love me. God has given me many gifts. I can do anything I want to if I make a plan, concentrate and work toward it every day.

# Sweet tea tastes best with a little lemon.

In our lives, both good and bad things happen around us. We have to deal with things that we do not enjoy.

We enjoy the good things in our life the most when we realize how good they are. One of the ways to realize how sweet something is, is to taste the opposite—something that's a little sour.

I am smart, happy and healthy. My parents love me. God has given me many gifts. I can do anything I want to if I make a plan, concentrate and work toward it every day.

There are two types of people in the world:
doers and watchers.

# If something important
# needs to be done, do it.

Doers are people who do things. They get things done.
They are the people who invent electricity, build houses,
write books and make beautiful music.

The watchers sit around and wait for the doers to invent or
build or fix things for them to enjoy. Practice being a doer
in the little things, and you will be a doer in the big things.

And if you are a watcher in the little things, you will
probably be a watcher in the big things.

I am smart, happy and healthy. My parents
love me. God has given me many gifts. I can do
anything I want to if I make a plan, concentrate
and work toward it every day.

# Look for the best in people.

When you first meet someone, there are two things you can do.

You could start looking for the things you think are wrong with them. Maybe they talk funny or you don't like their hair.

Or you could look for good things about the other person. Have they lived somewhere interesting? Do they play a musical instrument or sport that you like?

When you look for the good in someone, it helps people see the good in you. When you are always looking for the bad in others, it makes you look bad too.

Whether you are looking for the good or bad in others, you will probably find it.

I am smart, happy and healthy. My parents love me. God has given me many gifts. I can do anything I want to if I make a plan, concentrate and work toward it every day.

In life, sometimes 1 plus 1 equals 3.
That sounds weird, doesn't it?

Maybe one person can lift 25 pounds. Another person can also lift 25 pounds. But if those two people stand next to each other and work together, they might be able to lift 60 or 70 pounds—or maybe even 100 pounds. When two or more people

# work together

toward the same goal, they can do so much more than if each was working by himself.

Teamwork is powerful. If you can get along with other people and work well with them, you will be able to do so much more in life.

I am smart, happy and healthy. My parents love me. God has given me many gifts. I can do anything I want to if I make a plan, concentrate and work toward it every day.

# April 1st

The target isn't going to jump in front of your arrow. At times,

# everyone tries to do something and fails.

Maybe you're trying to learn how to do a double backflip or a new guitar chord—and it's tougher than it looks.

Don't get mad at someone else if you are having trouble learning something new or if things don't go the way you want them to. Usually it's not the other person's fault.

It's certainly not the guitar's fault.

When an archer shoots an arrow and misses the target, the archer must figure why he or she didn't shoot the arrow straight. Then the archer corrects the mistake and shoots again.

I am smart, happy and healthy. My parents love me. God has given me many gifts. I can do anything I want to if I make a plan, concentrate and work toward it every day.

We all have good days and bad days.

# Forgive people for their bad days.

Try to concentrate on the good things you do, not the bad. You should do the same thing for your friends and family, too.

Sometimes your dad or brother or sister might do something that upsets you. They probably aren't mad at you; they might just be having a bad day.

Try not to get mad at them. Forgive them for having a bad day. You would want them to do the same for you.

WHAT HAPPENED?!

I MISSED THE BUS AND IT STARTED RAINING.

I am smart, happy and healthy. My parents love me. God has given me many gifts. I can do anything I want to if I make a plan, concentrate and work toward it every day.

# Time is one of your most valuable assets.

There are a lot of things in life that you can earn, save, spend, play with and give away. But without time, none of these would be possible.

Don't waste your time.

You can't save time to use next week or next year like money. You can't give your time to someone else and let them have more of it.

You have to use your time right now, or you will lose it. It will be gone forever.

How will you spend your time today?

I am smart, happy and healthy. My parents love me. God has given me many gifts. I can do anything I want to if I make a plan, concentrate and work toward it every day.

# Guard your thoughts

like you would a precious safe full of valuables.

Your mind is like a safe full of precious jewels.
Everyone is trying to get into it. Some people
are trying to put things into your treasure box.
Other people are trying to take things out.

Only you know the combination. No matter how
hard other people try, you are responsible for
everything that goes into and comes out
of your wonderful mind.

You are responsible for protecting what
is in your mind. Do not let anyone inside
this vault without your permission.

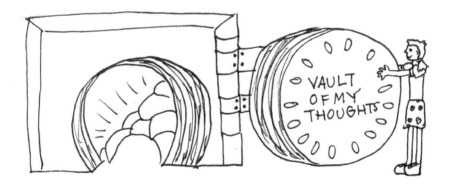

I am smart, happy and healthy. My parents
love me. God has given me many gifts. I can do
anything I want to if I make a plan, concentrate
and work toward it every day.

# You get to decide your own habits.

Habits are incredibly powerful things. When you don't think about your decisions, your habits are what make your decisions for you.

When people get older and have bad habits, a lot of times they try to change those habits. Maybe they eat the wrong food or don't exercise or use poor language. Those are habits. It is hard to change a habit, but it is easy to make a new one.

Right now you are making habits. Every time you do something, it is becoming a habit. If you want to have good habits when you are older, do good things now.

If you do bad things now, you will have bad habits when you get older.

I am smart, happy and healthy. My parents love me. God has given me many gifts. I can do anything I want to if I make a plan, concentrate and work toward it every day.

# Get better at something today.

Many people think that once they learn something they don't have to work on it any more. They believe that once they get out of school, they won't ever have to study again or do homework.

Those are very sad people.

Once you learn how to do something, that's when the learning really starts. You need to work every day to get better at the things you learn.

You never stay the same; you are always either getting better or getting worse.

The happiest people are the ones who learn things and get better at something their entire lives.

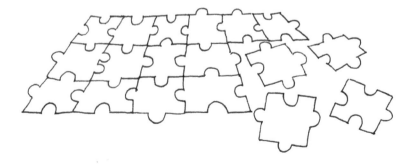

I am smart, happy and healthy. My parents love me. God has given me many gifts. I can do anything I want to if I make a plan, concentrate and work toward it every day.

# Anyone can become excited about an idea. Successful people stay excited.

If you really want to do something, work at it.
Work today, tomorrow and the next day.
If it is important to you, stay at it as long
as it takes, even if it takes years.

Everyone gets excited about ideas and wants to do
things. The people who actually do those things,
however, are the people who stay
committed to their goal long after they
first become excited about it.

I BUILT
REX'S NEW
DOG HOUSE!

I am smart, happy and healthy. My parents
love me. God has given me many gifts. I can do
anything I want to if I make a plan, concentrate
and work toward it every day.

# Everything and everyone is connected.

There are many ways that things can be connected. Your foot is connected to your leg by bones, skin and other gross looking stuff. The walls of your house are connected to the floor with nails.

Some connections in life aren't physical.

You are connected to your parents through the love you have for each other. This connection is just as real as the connection between your foot and your leg.

Your parents are connected to other people. Those other people are connected to the places they live and the nature around them. Through the connections we have, we reach out and touch everything else in the world.

I am smart, happy and healthy. My parents love me. God has given me many gifts. I can do anything I want to if I make a plan, concentrate and work toward it every day.

*April 9th*

When you
# share your fear
with someone else, the fear tends to disappear.

Everyone is afraid of something, even if they don't think about it all of the time. Maybe it's snakes. Or maybe you're afraid of cold doorknobs or balloons. Some people are even afraid of clowns!

If someone tells you he is afraid of bugs, you can explain that bugs aren't dangerous and that they are actually pretty cool if you get up close and look at them. That will probably help the person who is afraid of bugs.

If you are afraid of something, you will feel better if you tell someone and talk about it.

I am smart, happy and healthy. My parents love me. God has given me many gifts. I can do anything I want to if I make a plan, concentrate and work toward it every day.

It's better to never start something
than it is to quit before you finish.

# Don't begin a project unless you plan to finish it.

If it isn't important enough to finish,
then you shouldn't waste any time working
on it—not one day or one minute.

If it is important enough to finish,
then finish it. Make your plan, then
work on your plan until you are finished.

When you quit doing something before you
finish, you do at least two terrible things: one,
you don't finish the task. And two, you are
developing a habit of becoming a quitter.

I am smart, happy and healthy. My parents
love me. God has given me many gifts. I can do
anything I want to if I make a plan, concentrate
and work toward it every day.

# April 11th

If you are going to play,

# play to win.

Any time you are in a game, sport or any type of contest, it is important to treat the other person or team with respect. This is true whether you win or lose.

It is also important to enjoy yourself.

One of the best ways to enjoy yourself is to win. The only way to really win is to do your best.

If you are going to do anything, you should do your best. It is important to win—not because you want to beat the other guy, but because you have to do your best to win. All of us have to do that, and we always feel better when we do our best.

I am smart, happy and healthy. My parents love me. God has given me many gifts. I can do anything I want to if I make a plan, concentrate and work toward it every day.

# It takes two people to argue.

Unless you are a pretty weird person, it is impossible to get into an argument by yourself. Someone has to argue back. You can say mean things to someone, but if they don't say anything back, you won't end up in an argument. You will probably just get frustrated and walk away.

It's the same way if another person is saying the mean things. If you don't argue back, you won't get into an argument. The other person will probably get frustrated or bored and leave you alone.

If you are in an argument, it is *your* fault. No one can make you argue if you don't want to. Don't blame the other person.

I am smart, happy and healthy. My parents love me. God has given me many gifts. I can do anything I want to if I make a plan, concentrate and work toward it every day.

# Be a leader.

Every day in your life you are making decisions.
Little decisions and big decisions. What to eat.
What to wear. Will you be good to people?
Will you steal? Will you make good grades? Will you
do your responsibilities without being reminded?

Will you remember to go to the bathroom?

Who is going to make those decisions:
you, or someone else?

Of course you are going to make some of those
decisions; no one is going to tell you when to poop.

If you practice making decisions about little things
now, you will be able to make great decisions about
big things later.

You should be the one deciding. Be the leader.

GIRLS CAN PLAY FOOTBALL TOO!

I am smart, happy and healthy. My parents
love me. God has given me many gifts. I can do
anything I want to if I make a plan, concentrate
and work toward it every day.

# Enjoy the cruise, but drive the boat.

Life is a lot like driving a boat across a huge body of water. You are the captain. You can make the decisions to go in a certain direction, or you can just let the waves and wind decide where you go.

Sometimes the boat ride is smooth and other times the seas are rough. Even when the captain points the boat in the right direction, it is usually difficult to drive the boat in a straight line.

Like life, riding in the boat is more than half the fun. Lots of times there may be faster ways to get somewhere, but we choose to go on a boat because we want to enjoy the ride.

You are the captain. You get to make the decisions. Sometimes conditions outside your control will make things difficult for you, but if you quit driving the boat, the wind will probably blow you into the rocks.

I am smart, happy and healthy. My parents love me. God has given me many gifts. I can do anything I want to if I make a plan, concentrate and work toward it every day.

# *April 15th*

Trying to get something for nothing is the same thing as

# cheating or stealin g

Do you ever see people on the street begging and wonder why they don't spend their time and energy working? Many of them could probably earn the same amount of money or more. Are you ever tempted to ask or beg—or even scheme—for something rather than work for it?

Don't!

When you work for something, you have earned it and it is yours. When you beg for it, it really is not yours.

Begging is just a step or two away from stealing. Always work for your money and the other things you want in life.

I am smart, happy and healthy. My parents love me. God has given me many gifts. I can do anything I want to if I make a plan, concentrate and work toward it every day.

You won't miss any shots if you're sitting in the stands. But you won't score any points either.

When you try something new, there is a chance that you won't do as well as you hope to. When you first start a new hobby or skill, you won't be very good at it.

You might even be pretty bad at it.

Many people are too embarrassed to try something that they might not do well.

If everyone were that way, no one would ever try anything new. If babies were afraid to fall down, they would never learn to walk. They would crawl their whole lives. Get up. Walk.

# Get in the game. Take a shot.

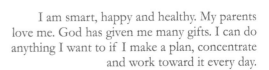

I am smart, happy and healthy. My parents love me. God has given me many gifts. I can do anything I want to if I make a plan, concentrate and work toward it every day.

# Everyone makes mistakes.

Have you ever done something that you wish you hadn't? It doesn't feel very good, does it? Maybe you hurt somebody or didn't do your homework when you should have.

You probably wanted forgiveness.

Believe it or not, everyone has those same kinds of things happen—even adults. Even parents!

Just as you need forgiveness when you make a mistake, so do other people.

I am smart, happy and healthy. My parents love me. God has given me many gifts. I can do anything I want to if I make a plan, concentrate and work toward it every day.

# Your mind is a muscle.

If you want strong arms or legs, you need to exercise those muscles. If you just sit around and don't do anything but eat potato chips and play video games all day, your body may get bigger, but you won't get any stronger.

Your mind is the same way. If you want it to get stronger, you have to use it. Like doing pushups or running in gym class, you have to keep trying and doing harder things for your brain to get smarter.

Read. Read a lot. Read new things. Ask questions. Search for answers. These are the ways you exercise the most important muscle in your body: your mind.

I am smart, happy and healthy. My parents love me. God has given me many gifts. I can do anything I want to if I make a plan, concentrate and work toward it every day.

If the decision is hard, ask yourself

# what would God want you to do?

Decisions can be hard. Sometimes even easy decisions might be a little tough, like what to eat for lunch.

But if you're struggling with a hard decision and can't figure out what to do, ask yourself one question: what would God want you to do?

This works really well when you're trying to decide really important questions like how to deal with people or how to use your time.

FLY AWAY
LITTLE BIRDY!

I am smart, happy and healthy. My parents love me. God has given me many gifts. I can do anything I want to if I make a plan, concentrate and work toward it every day.

# Decide to be happy today.

Did you read a book before going to bed last night? Did you
sing a song when you got up this morning, or just walk
downstairs? Did you hug your brother, sister or parents?

Whatever you did, you made a decision to do it or not to do it.

Being happy is the same way.

Most happy people decide that they want to be happy.
They work at it. When bad things happen, they
remind themselves: *I am a happy person.*

I am smart, happy and healthy. My parents
love me. God has given me many gifts. I can do
anything I want to if I make a plan, concentrate
and work toward it every day.

# *April 21st*

Birthday of Queen Elizabeth II of England
1926

# You say more with what you do

than what you say.

What would you think if your father
said he was the Queen of England?
You would probably think he was crazy.

But what if he wore a fancy robe and a
Queen's crown? What if he went around
England and people bowed in front of
him and said, "Hello, Queen"?

You might still think he was crazy, but it would
be just a tiny bit easier to believe that he might
be the Queen of England than if he just said it.

If you want people to know that you
are a good person, great student or
can play tennis or a musical instrument,
don't tell them. Show them.

I am smart, happy and healthy. My parents
love me. God has given me many gifts. I can do
anything I want to if I make a plan, concentrate
and work toward it every day.

# Just because your wheels are moving

doesn't mean you are going anywhere.

Sometimes people are busy, but they aren't doing anything really important. They might think they are, but really they are ignoring the things they should be doing. They are spending all of their time and energy on things that just aren't very important.

Maybe you are spending three hours every night brushing the dog's teeth. You tell your parents, "I'm very busy. Look, I'm working three hours every night."

But while you do that, you are skipping your homework, leaving your room a mess, and not spending any time with your friends or family.

You are driving really fast on the wrong road. You'll never get to where you are supposed to be.

I am smart, happy and healthy. My parents love me. God has given me many gifts. I can do anything I want to if I make a plan, concentrate and work toward it every day.

*April 23rd*

# Your friends feed your mind and soul.

Your mind is like a supercomputer that hears and records everything around it. Then it uses that information to make adjustments in you, changing the way you will be in the future.

Your friends have a lot to do with what information gets into your brain computer.

What do you think your friends will be doing when they get older? Will they be good students or bad students? Do you think they will be the kind of kids who get in trouble or not?

Whatever they are, you probably will be, too.

Decide what kind of person you want to be, then chose friends who are like that.

I am smart, happy and healthy. My parents love me. God has given me many gifts. I can do anything I want to if I make a plan, concentrate and work toward it every day.

# There is only one degree

of temperature difference between water and ice.

Water freezes at 32 degrees. At 33 degrees, it is water.
At 32 degrees or colder, it becomes hard ice.

If you are outside playing, can you tell the difference between 65 degrees and 66 degrees? Probably not. You can't tell the difference between 33 degrees and 32 degrees either. Yet that one degree of temperature is so powerful that it creates ice and snow. It creates dangers on the road, and it creates beauty in the mountains. That one degree of temperature is responsible for creating the beginnings of massive glaciers.

Our lives are the same way, except we don't know which degree will be responsible for the huge impact in our life. At some point in our life, it will take one more little degree of effort to make a huge change. We can turn our life from something soft like water, to something strong like ice…but we will have to find that last powerful degree of effort.

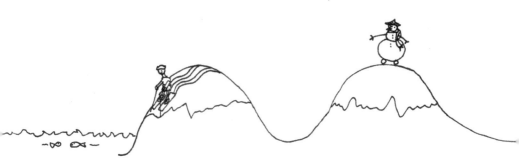

I am smart, happy and healthy. My parents love me. God has given me many gifts. I can do anything I want to if I make a plan, concentrate and work toward it every day.

# It is easier to win if you are used to winning.

To *motivate* someone means to help them find a way to be the best they can be. It means to help them win, or succeed.

The best motivator in the world is success.

The more you succeed, the easier it is to succeed the next time. If you get used to winning, you will win more than you lose. This sounds weird right now, but remember: the more you do something now, the more you will do it in the future.

I am smart, happy and healthy. My parents love me. God has given me many gifts. I can do anything I want to if I make a plan, concentrate and work toward it every day.

"Better three hours early than one minute late."
–Shakespeare

When you are early for church, a meeting, school or any
kind of appointment, it shows that you are prepared and
plan ahead. It means that you are organized.
It is a sign that you plan to be a successful person.

It also means that you respect the other people who will be
there. It is rude to make someone wait for you. It means
that you think their time isn't worth anything.
You think you are more important than them and they
should just sit around waiting for you.

# Plan. Be on time. Show that you respect people.

First Day of School

I am smart, happy and healthy. My parents
love me. God has given me many gifts. I can do
anything I want to if I make a plan, concentrate
and work toward it every day.

# *April 27th*

Birthday of Helen Keller
Highly accomplished deaf-mute
1880

# Don't become discouraged.

Helen Keller was a little girl who was
blind, deaf and couldn't talk. Yet she
learned to read by using a system of
touching letters with her fingers.
She learned to write.

She wrote many books that were a great
inspiration to the people who read them.
This girl had every reason in the world to be
frustrated and discouraged, but she took
advantage of the greatest tool in the world:
her mind! She used her mind to help
thousands and millions of others.

If you use your mind, anything is possible.

I am smart, happy and healthy. My parents
love me. God has given me many gifts. I can do
anything I want to if I make a plan, concentrate
and work toward it every day.

MONDAY

# **What you are** is not a sometime thing.

TUESDAY

Are you are hard worker? Are you honest? Are you a person who sets goals and makes plans?

Either you are or you aren't. It is impossible to be a hard worker just some of the time. You can't be a little honest. If you aren't honest, then you are dishonest.

An archer needs a straight arrow to be able to hit his target. An arrow can't be straight sometimes and crooked other times. Think about this: are you a boy or a girl? Can you be a boy sometimes and a girl sometimes? Of course not. Your character is the same way.

WEDNESDAY

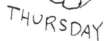

THURSDAY

FRIDAY

I am smart, happy and healthy. My parents love me. God has given me many gifts. I can do anything I want to if I make a plan, concentrate and work toward it every day.

# April 29th

Birthday of Baron Karl von Drais
Inventor of the bicycle
1785

You can't solve every situation by staying
in control. But you can make every
situation worse if you lose control.

If you are mad at your brother or sister and
yelling at them, are you getting anything done?
No, not really—except you may be
damaging your parents' ears.

Imagine you are riding a bicycle down a hill.
You are going so fast that you have lost control
of the pedals and can no longer steer the bike.
Is there any doubt how this will end?
You will crash.

If you are taking a test and run across several
difficult questions, does it do any good to get
upset and frustrated? Of course not.

# Stay in control.

I am smart, happy and healthy. My parents
love me. God has given me many gifts. I can do
anything I want to if I make a plan, concentrate
and work toward it every day.

The only way to get more is to

# give more.

This is a law of nature. It is as true as gravity.
It is just as certain as 2+2=4. You cannot receive
more in benefits and pleasure in life than
you are giving to others.

If you want more happiness, freedom or money
in your life, you have to help other people get
more of these things in their lives.

I am smart, happy and healthy. My parents
love me. God has given me many gifts. I can do
anything I want to if I make a plan, concentrate
and work toward it every day.

## May 1st

F.W. Rueckheim introduces Cracker Jacks
at the Chicago World's Fair
1893

Somewhere

# within every defeat
# is a secret prize.
# Find it.

Every time something bad happens, you have a
choice. You can be mad and upset, or you can try
to make something better from the situation.

Don't be one of the complainers.

Most people don't know the prize is within
every defeat. Very few people ever look for it. That
prize is the seed of something great. If you find
that seed, water it and take care of it, it will grow to
be bigger and better than you can imagine.

I am smart, happy and healthy. My parents
love me. God has given me many gifts. I can do
anything I want to if I make a plan, concentrate
and work toward it every day.

Only look backwards if you want to go that way.

When your parents are driving a car, the only time they turn around and look out the rear window is when they are backing up. Most of the time they look out the windshield, so they can see where they are going.

Life should be lived the same way.

If you spend all your time looking back—that is, thinking about things that have already happened—you won't be able to concentrate on where you want to go.

You might even crash.

# Look in the direction you want to go.

I am smart, happy and healthy. My parents love me. God has given me many gifts. I can do anything I want to if I make a plan, concentrate and work toward it every day.

*May 3rd*

# Be willing
to do things that most people won't do.

When there is a hard or yucky chore to do around the
house, who usually does it? Your mother? Your father?

You should offer to do these chores. An even better idea
would be to go ahead and do them without being asked.

When you do things that others aren't willing to do,
you show that you are responsible. You show that
you are mature.

People who do more yucky things in life without being
asked usually get to do more fun things too.

I am smart, happy and healthy. My parents
love me. God has given me many gifts. I can do
anything I want to if I make a plan, concentrate
and work toward it every day.

# Always do what you say you are going to do.

There are two good things that will happen when you always do what you say you will do. First, people will always believe you. It is easier to do great things in life if people believe you. The most important reason to always do what you say you are going to do is that you will always believe yourself. Lying to yourself is the most dangerous kind of lie to tell.

If you can't trust yourself, no one else will trust you, either.

I am smart, happy and healthy. My parents love me. God has given me many gifts. I can do anything I want to if I make a plan, concentrate and work toward it every day.

There is a difference between

# a hope, a dream and a goal.

Sometimes we say we want something, but we don't really do anything to get it. If you are hungry, do you go outside, look up at the sky, open your mouth and hope God drops some dinner in there?

No. You decide what you want, then cook it. Before that you had to go to the grocery store. And before that, you had to make enough money to buy groceries.

You had a real plan for your meals. You weren't just hoping that you would get food.

All of life works that way.

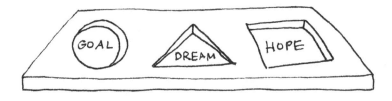

I am smart, happy and healthy. My parents love me. God has given me many gifts. I can do anything I want to if I make a plan, concentrate and work toward it every day.

# Always be honest.

There are lots of different ways to be dishonest.
Telling a lie is one of them. But so is cheating.
So is stealing. So is blaming someone else
for your mistake.

Being lazy is also dishonest.
You are dishonest if you don't do your best.

Always tell the truth. Always be honest.
And always do your best.

I am smart, happy and healthy. My parents
love me. God has given me many gifts. I can do
anything I want to if I make a plan, concentrate
and work toward it every day.

# Most problems can be solved if you keep working at them in the right way.

Everyone has things that don't go right in their life. Maybe something breaks. Or perhaps they are having trouble learning to play a musical instrument, a new sport or something in school.

Throughout your life, there will always be things that are hard.

Some people will never solve those problems. Other people, however, always seem to solve their problems. What is the difference?

The people who solve their problems are the ones who don't give up.

If the solution doesn't come easily, they try something else. Or they try harder. They don't quit.

I am smart, happy and healthy. My parents love me. God has given me many gifts. I can do anything I want to if I make a plan, concentrate and work toward it every day.

# Cooperation creates power.

When you cooperate with someone it means that you work together to try to achieve a goal. Maybe you are helping someone build a fence or clean the house. Whatever it is, when you help someone, it also helps you.

Some day you are going to need to do things that you can't do by yourself. You are going to need people to help you. Maybe you will be president of a company or the country and will need lots of people to help you.

If you learn how to work with cooperation, you will have the power to do those big jobs.

KIDS ONLY!

I am smart, happy and healthy. My parents love me. God has given me many gifts. I can do anything I want to if I make a plan, concentrate and work toward it every day.

There
is usually no such
thing as *can't.*

# There is only *won't.*

Many people will try something and if it doesn't work out for them they say, "I can't do that." Sometimes they might say it before they even try it. They just decide that it is too hard or too complicated for them. Maybe they are too lazy to try. So they say, "I can't do that." What they are usually really saying is "I won't do that" or "I don't want to do that." People can do so much more than they think they can—if they will just push themselves. Push. Try hard. When you think you've done all that you can do, then try even harder. What you can do will amaze you.

I am smart, happy and healthy. My parents love me. God has given me many gifts. I can do anything I want to if I make a plan, concentrate and work toward it every day.

You eat a bear the same way you
eat a piece of apple pie:

# one bite at a time.

Sometimes when you start work on something
the job seems so large that you think it
will take forever to get it done.

If the job is that big, you'd better get started.

You could eat a whole bear if you wanted to,
but it would take a very long time. The longer
you waited to get started, however, the older you
would be when you finished.

It's just like reading a huge book.
You read it one page at a time.

# May 11th

It's hard to be really good at something unless you

# have fun doing it.

When you are deciding what kinds of activities you want to do, remember that you are going to be best at something you enjoy doing. That just makes sense. If you like playing basketball or writing stories, you will want to do it a lot—and that will make you better at it.

Remember this when you get a job as a grown-up. If you pick a job or business that you really love, you will be better at it than at a job you hate. Life is short; pick things to do that you enjoy doing.

I am smart, happy and healthy. My parents love me. God has given me many gifts. I can do anything I want to if I make a plan, concentrate and work toward it every day.

# Write down your thoughts.

When you write something down, it forces you to concentrate on your ideas. Sometimes it makes us more organized in the way we put our plans together.

It also gives us a record of our thoughts over time. This will allow you to go back and see how you have changed your thinking, goals and dreams over the years.

I am smart, happy and healthy. My parents love me. God has given me many gifts. I can do anything I want to if I make a plan, concentrate and work toward it every day.

# If you love someone, do something for them

that they could do for themselves.

It's easy to do something for someone who needs your help. Good people help those around them who are in need.

If you do something that they could do themselves—maybe just a little favor—that is a special act of love. Think of the people you love today. What can you do for them that would be special?

I am smart, happy and healthy. My parents love me. God has given me many gifts. I can do anything I want to if I make a plan, concentrate and work toward it every day.

## May 14th

If you want to do something,
you must first be able to

# see yourself doing it in your mind.

Your mind is the most powerful and magical
movie theater in the world. The movies you
play on the theater in your mind can help you
see things that might happen in the future.

One thing is sure: if you aren't confident enough
in your plans or goals to be able to see yourself
doing it on the big screen in your mind, it will
never happen in real life.

All great things start as a thought.
Then they become a vision in your mind.

Only then can they become reality.

I am smart, happy and healthy. My parents
love me. God has given me many gifts. I can do
anything I want to if I make a plan, concentrate
and work toward it every day.

# Don't waste your thoughts.

Each day has 1,440 minutes. What if each thought takes one minute? If you sleep eight hours a day, at most you can have only 960 thoughts each day.

Every time you have a negative thought, you are taking away the opportunity to have a good one. You are wasting a thought. You are wasting a resource that you can never get back.

Negative thoughts attract negative outcomes. Positive thoughts attract positive outcomes.

Which do you want to attract?

I am smart, happy and healthy. My parents love me. God has given me many gifts. I can do anything I want to if I make a plan, concentrate and work toward it every day.

# No one can read your mind.

Tell people what you want. Ask people for their help. Thank them if they do it. If you do these things, people will want to help you more.

Sometimes you may think your parents know what you want or that you need something. They may be smart, but they can't read your mind.

Tell them.

People love to be thanked and praised; they will do more things to get your praise.

Reward people for great behavior—even adults!

I WOULD LIKE A GUITAR FOR MY BIRTHDAY.

I am smart, happy and healthy. My parents love me. God has given me many gifts. I can do anything I want to if I make a plan, concentrate and work toward it every day.

# Doing is better than planning or talking.

Lots of people *talk* about what they are going to *do*. Some people actually make plans. Talking is okay. Planning is better than talking.

Don't talk about doing it, or just plan. Do it.

Do your homework. Clean your room. Practice your guitar. Build a fort. Paint a picture. Write a story. It's always better to *do* than to *talk* about doing.

I am smart, happy and healthy. My parents love me. God has given me many gifts. I can do anything I want to if I make a plan, concentrate and work toward it every day.

# You can't keep a bird from pooping on your head,

but you don't have to leave it there.

If a bird flew over your head just as he was using the bathroom, what would you do? Be depressed? Go to school the next day and show everyone the bird poop on your head?

No. You would clean it off.

When bad things happen, try not to get mad about it.

 You can get mad at the bird, but he is already gone. When bad things happen, clean up the mess.

I am smart, happy and healthy. My parents love me. God has given me many gifts. I can do anything I want to if I make a plan, concentrate and work toward it every day.

# May 19th

"If I could do anything I would _____."

How did you fill in the blank? That's your dream.

Think carefully about answering the question, because if you know what to do with your dreams, they just might come true.

Dream big. You get to fill in the blanks with anything you want.

# Don't settle

for something small.

Someone has to do big things. Why not you?

GO ON AN ADVENTURE!!!

I am smart, happy and healthy. My parents love me. God has given me many gifts. I can do anything I want to if I make a plan, concentrate and work toward it every day.

When you put your mind on something,

# there is an invisible force

that draws that thing to you.

If you spend all day thinking about books,
you will probably read more books and
write more stories and letters.

If you spend all day thinking about food,
you will probably eat more.

It is hard to explain, but this power of your mind is
just as certain and just as powerful as the gravity
that holds us all on the earth, keeping us from
flying off as the world spins each day.

I am smart, happy and healthy. My parents
love me. God has given me many gifts. I can do
anything I want to if I make a plan, concentrate
and work toward it every day.

# Wanting to win is easy;

wanting to prepare to win is hard.

No one wants to lose. Winning is fun. Everyone wants to be a winner. At least everyone says they want to be a winner.

People who really want to win, however, will be just as excited about something else: doing all the work that is needed to have a chance to win. The work is hard, but that is what actually makes a winner. It is also what most people don't do. They just say they want to win, then don't do what is necessary to win.

They don't really want to win.

I am smart, happy and healthy. My parents love me. God has given me many gifts. I can do anything I want to if I make a plan, concentrate and work toward it every day.

# You have to be ready for good luck.

A lot of things in our lives seem to happen for no reason. Maybe you get a part in a play or a position on a team. Or maybe you win a contest at school.

You have a part in making each of those things happen.

Life presents us opportunities every day. A contest at school is an opportunity. So is an audition or trying out for a sports team. But those opportunities are lost if you don't do the work to be ready for them.

When you stay prepared, good luck has an easier time finding you.

FOUND YOU!

I am smart, happy and healthy. My parents love me. God has given me many gifts. I can do anything I want to if I make a plan, concentrate and work toward it every day.

# You can do more than you think you can.

Most of the
good things in life
take hard work. Good
grades, good relationships,
a good job or business. If
you want to be a great student,
musician or athlete you have
to work very hard.

Most people never become great
because they don't work hard at it. They say
they work hard. They may even think they work
hard. But when you've worked as hard as you think
you can at something you care about, don't stop. That's
when you must do more. That's when you must find that
extra strength inside you that helps make you great.

It's like hiking a mountain. Just when you think you're out of
energy and can't walk any more, that's when you have to push
yourself and reach the top.

I am smart, happy and healthy. My parents
love me. God has given me many gifts. I can do
anything I want to if I make a plan, concentrate
and work toward it every day.

# Do the things you are supposed to do

before doing the things you want to do.

Everyone has two types of tasks: things they are supposed to do and things they want to do. Always do the things you are supposed to do first.

These are your responsibilities. These are things like making your bed, doing homework, feeding the animals, doing a school report and cleaning the house.

Don't go outside and play until you get those responsibilities done. Your responsibilities are the most important things. Always do them first.

I am smart, happy and healthy. My parents love me. God has given me many gifts. I can do anything I want to if I make a plan, concentrate and work toward it every day.

# What are you going to do when you get hurt?

Cry and whine? Or be tough?

Things are going to happen in your life that will hurt. You might drop a frozen turkey on your toe and break it. (Your toe, not the turkey.)

Somebody might say something mean to you. That would hurt, but in a different way.

Be tough. Whining or complaining is just a way to feel sorry for yourself, and that just makes you weak. And the weaker you are the more likely you are to get hurt again.

When you are tough, the hurt doesn't hurt as long or as badly.

I am smart, happy and healthy. My parents love me. God has given me many gifts. I can do anything I want to if I make a plan, concentrate and work toward it every day.

Practice doesn't make perfect.

# Practice makes permanent.

Many people believe that "practice makes perfect." Not true. You will only become perfect from your practice if you are perfect in your practice.

Athletes can't just show up at practice and hope they get better. They will play the way they practice.

There is a guarantee, however. Whatever you do every day will become your habit. The more you do something—or practice it—the more permanent that thing will be in your personality.

I am smart, happy and healthy. My parents love me. God has given me many gifts. I can do anything I want to if I make a plan, concentrate and work toward it every day.

*May 27th*

# Lemonade tastes best with a little sugar.

Although most people like lemonade, you have probably never seen anyone walking around sucking on a lemon. Lemons are sour.

In order to make a tasty drink, we usually add a little bit of something sweet to the recipe.

Life is the same way.

A lot of things in life are sour. If you concentrate on those sour things, you will probably walk around with a puckered look on your face, just as if you were sucking on a lemon.

If you think about some of the good things around you, however, that is the "sweetness" in the recipe of your life.

Just as sweet tea tastes best with a little lemon, by joining the hard things with the sweet things in your life, you will have an amazing and enjoyable combination.

I am smart, happy and healthy. My parents love me. God has given me many gifts. I can do anything I want to if I make a plan, concentrate and work toward it every day.

# Most people never really push themselves.

How much can you do? More.

When you are working hard at a project
and come to a difficult part, what do you do?
If you are like most people, you try harder.

That's right, most people try harder
when things first get tough. But if things stay
difficult for long, most people quit trying
harder. Or they just completely quit.

Winners are people who push themselves. They
get up earlier and work harder than others.
They sweat when other people are resting.

They find the energy to do what other people
don't even realize is possible.

I am smart, happy and healthy. My parents
love me. God has given me many gifts. I can do
anything I want to if I make a plan, concentrate
and work toward it every day.

# Be patient.

The best things can take a long time.

Some day you will want to buy something
expensive like a car. How should you pay for it? Save
the money. It might take you several years to get enough.

Every time you get some money, however, you might want to
spend it all going to a movie. Or buying a book.
Or maybe getting a new pair of pants.

All of those things would be fun, but if you always spend
your money on a bunch of small things, you will never
save enough to buy a big thing.

Most things in life are like that—not just things that cost
money. You might have to work on some goals for years,
even though it might be more fun today just to watch TV.

Sometimes the best things take time.

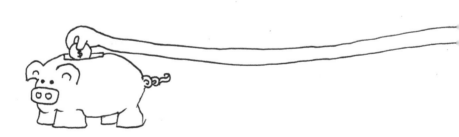

I am smart, happy and healthy. My parents
love me. God has given me many gifts. I can do
anything I want to if I make a plan, concentrate
and work toward it every day.

If you want people to respect you, you have to

# show respect to others.

It's hard to ask someone to give you something if you're not willing to give them the same thing. Why would someone be nice to you if you weren't nice to them?

You might ask someone for a glass of water. What if you had ignored them every time they asked you for some water?

You would probably be pretty thirsty.

To respect someone means that you treat them like they are important. *Everyone* is important, including you, so be sure to treat everyone that way.

I am smart, happy and healthy. My parents love me. God has given me many gifts. I can do anything I want to if I make a plan, concentrate and work toward it every day.

# There is only one person you should try to control: you.

A lot of times you might want someone to act differently. Maybe you want your brother or sister to quit bothering you. Or you want your parents to quit telling you to do your homework every afternoon.

If you try to get the other person to change, two things might happen. There's a good chance you will fail, and that won't make you happy. And the person you are trying to change or control will get upset with you, too. Quit trying to get the other person to change.

The best thing to do is to try to change yourself. If you can't change or control the other person, change the way you react to them.

You *can* control that.

THEIR
TOMFOOLERY
ISN'T GOING
TO BOTHER
ME ANYMORE.

I am smart, happy and healthy. My parents love me. God has given me many gifts. I can do anything I want to if I make a plan, concentrate and work toward it every day.

If you want to change the way you are feeling,

# change the way you are acting.

If you're sad or mad or upset about something,
pretend you are happy, even if you aren't.
Make yourself smile, even if you don't feel like
it. Stand up straight, even if you really feel like
slouching. Speak in a strong, but calm voice,
even if you feel like crying.

It is impossible for your mind and body to
disagree with each other.

I am smart, happy and healthy. My parents
love me. God has given me many gifts. I can do
anything I want to if I make a plan, concentrate
and work toward it every day.

# There is an order to the universe.

Everything in the world is connected in an unseen, magical way. People, animals, the mountains, rivers, oceans, air... when something affects one of these things, it has an effect on all of those things. If you do something mean to anyone or anything, it hurts the entire universe. You kill a little of your soul and you hurt a little of everyone else's, too. When you do something to help another person, it has a positive impact on the whole universe. it makes the energy of the world more positive.

I am smart, happy and healthy. My parents love me. God has given me many gifts. I can do anything I want to if I make a plan, concentrate and work toward it every day.

# You can't always agree with everyone.

That doesn't mean that you have to fight with them.

The people you will disagree with more than anyone else are the people you are around most. That usually includes some of your close friends and people in your family.

That's okay. There is nothing wrong with not agreeing about something.

Not agreeing about something, however, doesn't mean that you have to argue or fight about it. You don't have to convince others that they are wrong, even if you are convinced they are wrong.

Learn to disagree with people without fighting with them. You will be much happier…and so will the other person.

I am smart, happy and healthy. My parents love me. God has given me many gifts. I can do anything I want to if I make a plan, concentrate and work toward it every day.

# If you are healthy, you can do almost anything.

If you are not healthy, you can do almost nothing.

There are several parts to being healthy. Obviously, you need to take care of your body. Eat right. Play outside. Exercise. Don't sit around watching TV all the time.

You need to exercise your mind and spirit to keep them healthy, too. How do you do that?

Read. Pray. Meditate. Play games that make you think. Work to make all A's in class.

When your whole person is healthy—your body, mind and spirit—you are able to concentrate on your goals and plans. And you will have the strength to work on those goals and plans every day.

I am smart, happy and healthy. My parents love me. God has given me many gifts. I can do anything I want to if I make a plan, concentrate and work toward it every day.

# If you don't get started you won't get finished.

The biggest reason most people fail at things is that they never start. They never start to set goals. They never make a plan.

They never start work on a huge project at school.

They never start reading a book or maybe even writing a book.

There are plenty of reasons people might not finish something. They might get distracted. They might not be able to do it. It might be too hard for them.

But one thing that will always cause someone to fail is to simply never start.

I am smart, happy and healthy. My parents love me. God has given me many gifts. I can do anything I want to if I make a plan, concentrate and work toward it every day.

# June 6th

Anniversary of U.S. military
landing at Normandy, France
1944

# The greatest sacrifice
# a person can make
# is for a stranger.

A sacrifice is when you give away something
important to try to help another person. Parents
sacrifice things like their time, or maybe even
their health, for their children.

Sometimes, however, people will make a sacrifice to help
someone they don't know. Maybe you see a broken part
on the swing set at a park and fix it so no one will get
hurt after you leave.

One group of strangers who made a huge sacrifice for you
are the men and women in the military who fought in wars
to protect our country and keep us safe from evil people
who want to change our way of life. These soldiers
fought—and many of them died—so we can enjoy
freedoms that allow us to do almost anything we want to do.

They made the biggest sacrifice—all for strangers.

I am smart, happy and healthy. My parents
love me. God has given me many gifts. I can do
anything I want to if I make a plan, concentrate
and work toward it every day.

# Clothes do *not* make the man.

The way something looks on the outside doesn't tell you what's on the inside. Like a book cover, a person might wear boring clothes and look boring on the outside until you get to know them or start reading their book.

Sometimes it is tempting to choose friends simply because of how they look.

How sad.

A sign of a mature person is choosing people to be your friends because they make you a better person—not because you like the way they look.

HEY GUYS !

I am smart, happy and healthy. My parents love me. God has given me many gifts. I can do anything I want to if I make a plan, concentrate and work toward it every day.

# Everything starts as a thought.

Before someone could build the first car, he first had the idea. The same is true of a book; all books begin in the mind of an author.

Roads, the U.S. Constitution, Walt Disney World, television shows...each of these started in the thoughts of the people who created them.

Thoughts are powerful things. They are the beginning point of everything in our lives.

I am smart, happy and healthy. My parents love me. God has given me many gifts. I can do anything I want to if I make a plan, concentrate and work toward it every day.

# Focus on what you do want,

not what you don't want.

When we put our mind on something,
we start to move in that direction.

If you are riding a bicycle and look over your left
shoulder, your bicycle will start to move to the
left, even if you don't want it to. It just happens.

Our life is the same way, so be careful what
you think about. If you want to have better
handwriting, don't tell yourself, "I don't want
to have messy handwriting." Tell yourself,
"I am going to have great handwriting."

You want your mind to hear
"great handwriting" not "messy handwriting."

Think about moving toward the positive,
not away from the negative.

I am smart, happy and healthy. My parents
love me. God has given me many gifts. I can do
anything I want to if I make a plan, concentrate
and work toward it every day.

# Attitude is everything.

The man or woman who can control their attitude can accomplish almost anything. The person with no control of their attitude can accomplish almost nothing.

Your attitude affects everything you touch in your life. A positive attitude will help you at school and at home. You can study better and it's easier to do homework with a great attitude.

It's also a lot easier to get along with others.

With a bad attitude, everything is harder. It will be harder to focus on your schoolwork or play. You will get into arguments. No one will want to be around you.

Choose to have a great attitude today.

I am smart, happy and healthy. My parents love me. God has given me many gifts. I can do anything I want to if I make a plan, concentrate and work toward it every day.

# When you go fishing, use bait that fish like.

Different things are important to different people. Not everyone is the same.

When you go fishing, why don't you put pizza on your hook? Because fish like worms more than they like pizza.

If you want to attract another person or get their attention, think about what that person might like. It's probably different from your favorite things.

People are different from fish. And they are often different from each other, too.

I am smart, happy and healthy. My parents love me. God has given me many gifts. I can do anything I want to if I make a plan, concentrate and work toward it every day.

*June 12th*

# Kindness and meanness are both big things.

When you surprise someone with something nice, it usually makes a big impact on them. If they don't expect it, you will probably help them have a great day, and that may inspire them to help someone else have a great day.

When you do a mean thing it works the same way. That person might spend the rest of their day doing mean things to people.

I am smart, happy and healthy. My parents love me. God has given me many gifts. I can do anything I want to if I make a plan, concentrate and work toward it every day.

# You will never do more than you can dream.

When you use your imagination to think about what you might do in life or what goals you want to achieve, you are planting seeds in your mind.

Just planting a seed won't make fruit grow, but if you don't plant a seed, you will never get the fruit.

Dream big. The dream is a seed. Plant great seeds and, if you water and take care of those seeds, you will have a chance to have great fruit.

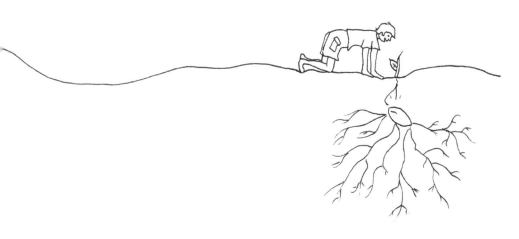

I am smart, happy and healthy. My parents love me. God has given me many gifts. I can do anything I want to if I make a plan, concentrate and work toward it every day.

# A good idea without *action* is worthless.

How many times have you ever thought of a plan, game or something to do that you thought was a good idea? Did you actually *do* the idea, or just talk about it?

Lots of people have ideas that would be great if they would only do something with those ideas. The best thing to do with a good idea is to act on it.

I am smart, happy and healthy. My parents love me. God has given me many gifts. I can do anything I want to if I make a plan, concentrate and work toward it every day.

# When you give a gift it creates a connection

between you and the other person.

There are many types of gifts you can give a person.

You can give an actual item—something in a box. Or you can write a poem or story. You might draw a picture or make something. Or you could simply give your time and help a person do something.

No matter what type of gift you give a person, it will always make the other person feel good. It will also make you feel good. A gift, when given in happiness, lifts the spirit of both the person getting and receiving the gift.

Give to others.

I am smart, happy and healthy. My parents love me. God has given me many gifts. I can do anything I want to if I make a plan, concentrate and work toward it every day.

# Everyone has a talent.

If you want to be happy, use that talent.

The happiest people are the ones who are doing something they enjoy. People are usually better at things they enjoy.

That doesn't mean that you should be an expert the first time you try to sing, play baseball, tumble or do math. But there are things that you can naturally do better than other things. There are also things that you enjoy doing more than other things.

If you concentrate doing those things that you enjoy and that you can do well, you will be very good at them—and you are more likely to be happy doing them.

I am smart, happy and healthy. My parents
love me. God has given me many gifts.
I can do anything I want to if I make a plan,
concentrate and work toward it every day.

# Don't wait

until it starts raining to start fixing the roof.

If you are working on a hole in your roof during a rainstorm, all of the stuff in the house is already getting wet. You probably aren't doing a very good job of working on the roof either. Fix the roof as soon as you realize it needs to be repaired.

Plan ahead. If you don't plan ahead, you will always be reacting to things. You can't make good decisions when you are reacting. If you plan ahead, you won't be rushed.

This is true for your schoolwork. Do your homework early. If you have a project, do it as soon as your teacher gives it to you; don't wait until the day or two before it is due.

I am smart, happy and healthy. My parents love me. God has given me many gifts. I can do anything I want to if I make a plan, concentrate and work toward it every day.

*June 18th*

When something doesn't go your way, ask yourself,

# "What am I supposed to learn from this?"

When you are disappointed about something,
it might seem as if nothing ever goes your way. That's
not true, but it can feel that way.

Use that feeling to learn something,
or the bad feeling will be wasted.

Did you make a mistake? Did someone else
make a mistake? Are you learning how to
change plans when you hadn't planned to?
Maybe your disappointment is a challenge
to teach you not to give up.

Whatever it is, look for it. There is **always**
a lesson in every disappointment.

I am smart, happy and healthy. My parents
love me. God has given me many gifts. I can do
anything I want to if I make a plan, concentrate
and work toward it every day.

Don't brag about yourself.

# Brag about others.

When you tell everyone how good you are at baseball or playing a musical instrument, that usually means that you are afraid the other person doesn't like you or doesn't think you are "good enough" in some way. You are trying to make yourself look better.

It actually does the opposite. When you try to make yourself look big by bragging, it makes you look smaller.

When you brag about other people, however, it makes you look big. It makes it look like you are so comfortable with your own accomplishments that you don't have to talk about them. You want to lift other people up because you don't have to lift up yourself.

Brag about others. It's good for both of you.

MARCELLA IS ONE OF THE BEST CHEERLEADERS ON THE SQUAD

I am smart, happy and healthy. My parents love me. God has given me many gifts. I can do anything I want to if I make a plan, concentrate and work toward it every day.

# Never feel
# sorry for yourself.

It won't help anything.

People might feel sorry for themselves for lots of reasons.
Maybe you wanted something that you didn't get. Maybe
someone got mad at you. Maybe somebody hurt your feelings.

If something like that happens, you can't change it.
All you can do is decide how to react to it.

If you try to stay positive, maybe the negative
spirit of that disappointment won't stick to you.

But if you feel sorry for yourself, you are
guaranteed to feel worse.

I am smart, happy and healthy. My parents
love me. God has given me many gifts. I can do
anything I want to if I make a plan, concentrate
and work toward it every day.

HAMLETCAST

| | |
|---|---|
| CLAUDIUS | Morgan |
| HAMLET | Hudson |
| POLONIUS | Brandon |
| HORATIO | Derrick |
| LAERTES | Caroline |
| LUCIANUS | Kayla |
| VOLTIMAND | Zack |
| CORNELIUS | Dennis |
| ROSENCRANTZ | Glenn |
| GUILDENSTERN | Sien |

NO WORRIES,
ILL TRY AGAIN
NEXT YEAR.

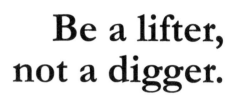

# Be a lifter, not a digger.

Everyone has an impact on other people. You influence your friends, teachers, parents, brother and sister. You influence everyone around you in some way.

Here is the important question: do you lift their spirits? Or do you dig a hole for their spirits to fall in?

Are you a lifter or a digger?

Be a lifter and try to be around other lifters.

I am smart, happy and healthy. My parents love me. God has given me many gifts. I can do anything I want to if I make a plan, concentrate and work toward it every day.

## June 22nd

# You get to decide your future. No one else.

If you want something to happen in your life, don't hope for it. Don't wish for it.

Decide for it.

*You can do anything you want to do if you make a plan, if you concentrate and if you work toward it every day.*

What word do you keep seeing? **"You."** **You** are the one who has to make a plan. **You** are the one who has to concentrate. **You** are the one who has to do the work.

No one else is going to do it.
It is not going to happen by accident.

You get to decide what you are going to have and do with your life.

I am smart, happy and healthy. My parents love me. God has given me many gifts. I can do anything I want to if I make a plan, concentrate and work toaward it every day.

At the end of each day,
spend one minute thinking about

# the best thing that happened that day.

Sometimes it is easy to forget all of the good things that happen in our lives. We get busy thinking about what's happening now, or maybe something that happened to upset us.

The best thing for our spirit, however, is to concentrate on our good times.

What was the best thing that happened today? Did you do something to help put a smile on someone's face? Did someone help put a smile on your face?

Did you achieve a goal you had set for yourself? Was there a special time today where you felt God in your life?

Spend a minute or two every night just before you go to sleep thinking about the best part of your day. You will go to sleep happier. You will wake up that way, too.

I am smart, happy and healthy. My parents love me. God has given me many gifts. I can do anything I want to if I make a plan, concentrate and work toward it every day.

# Thoughts are things.

When you hold a rock or book it is easy to feel and see that those objects are real things. You can hold a rock. One person can give a book to another person.

Believe it or not, thoughts are also things.

You can hold them, but not in your hands. You hold them in your mind. You hold them in your heart. You can give your thoughts to other people.

In your hand, a rock, a book or almost anything else can be powerful. You can use it for good or evil.

Thoughts are the same way, so be careful what thoughts you carry around with you and how you use them.

I am smart, happy and healthy. My parents love me. God has given me many gifts. I can do anything I want to if I make a plan, concentrate and work toward it every day.

# If you have to swallow a frog,

don't stare at it too long.

Sometimes we have to do things that we don't want to. Even though it may be gross or seem impossible, it may be something we absolutely have to do.

If so, don't put it off. Just do it.

The longer we wait, the more we will dread it. The more we dread it, the more energy we are wasting that we could be spending on things that we would enjoy.

Don't put off doing the hard things. You will be much happier if you get them done.

I am smart, happy and healthy. My parents love me. God has given me many gifts. I can do anything I want to if I make a plan, concentrate and work toward it every day.

# Honesty

only matters when it
matters, which is every time.

There are a lot of times in life that you can do
little wrongs and no one but you will know about them.

In those situations, there seem to be no terrible consequences
if you tell a little lie or do some small wrong to a person.

Until someone finds out.

That one time the person finds out you have been dishonest,
you will lose their trust. They may be angry…very angry. They
may never want to be around you again. You might get kicked
out of school, go to jail or even worse. The scary thing is that
you never know when that time will be. Any small dishonesty
might have all of these terrible consequences.

So you must treat every situation as if it is the most important
situation in your life, and always act honestly.

I'M SORRY,
I FORGOT
TO PUT
DIAMOND
AWAY.

I am smart, happy and healthy. My parents
love me. God has given me many gifts. I can do
anything I want to if I make a plan, concentrate
and work toward it every day.

# Being lazy hurts

the people around you, but it hurts you more.

If you have responsibilities and you are too lazy to do them, you aren't pulling your weight. If you don't make your bed or clean your room, this hurts your parents. If you are on a sports team and don't do what you are supposed to, this hurts all your teammates.

However, another thing happens when you're lazy. You get in the habit of not doing your responsibilities. Every time you're lazy, it makes it a little easier to be lazy the next time.

This hurts you in every part of your life. It is worse for you than anyone else.

I am smart, happy and healthy. My parents love me. God has given me many gifts. I can do anything I want to if I make a plan, concentrate and work toward it every day.

# Money can't buy happiness.

Some people think money is the most important thing in the world.

They are wrong.

The most important thing in the world is *people*. Relationships are important. True friends are important. Love is important. Friendship and love are gifts that you give to others, and the gifts they give to you.

You can use money to buy lots of things—like tennis rackets, school supplies, houses or books—and there's nothing wrong with that.

But money cannot make a person happy.

*family is happiest*

I am smart, happy and healthy. My parents love me. God has given me many gifts. I can do anything I want to if I make a plan, concentrate and work toward it every day.

# If you help other people

get what they want in life, it will become
easier to get what you want.

There is nothing wrong with wanting things.
Everyone should have goals. You might
be surprised, however, at one of the best
ways to get the things you want.

Help other people get the things they want.

So if you aren't getting the things you
wish you had, maybe you should find
someone you can help. You will be blessed.

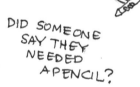

DID SOMEONE
SAY THEY
NEEDED
A PENCIL?

I am smart, happy and healthy. My parents
love me. God has given me many gifts. I can do
anything I want to if I make a plan, concentrate
and work toward it every day.

*June 30th*

**Dreams**

are where good
things start, not end.

Dreams are great. In dreams, we think
of things we might never imagine
when we are awake. Some people have
daydreams, where they let their minds
think of wonderful and exciting things
they have never experienced.

But if all you do is dream, you will
never live those wonderful
experiences. Some people have great
dreams, but those dreams aren't
worth anything until they begin to
make a plan and work toward making
those dreams come true.

Take action toward your dreams today.

I am smart, happy and healthy. My parents
love me. God has given me many gifts. I can do
anything I want to if I make a plan, concentrate
and work toward it every day.

# God may give you the wisdom

to answer your questions,
but he is not going to give you a pony.

At the end or beginning of each day, you probably
pray and ask God to help you with things. Maybe you
ask God to give you certain things.

That's okay, but don't sit around and just wait for God
to take care of things for you. If you ask and listen,
God will help you find answers to your questions. But
if you want something to happen, you have to do it;
no one will just do it for you, not even God.

You are responsible for what happens to you.

I am smart, happy and healthy. My parents
love me. God has given me many gifts. I can do
anything I want to if I make a plan, concentrate
and work toward it every day.

# When you have a thought you are starting a process

that determines what kind of person you will become.

Thoughts affect what you say. What you say affects what you do.

What you do eventually becomes your habit. Habits are the things you do without thinking about them.

And your habits are who you are.

So be careful what you think about, because that is what you will become.

I am smart, happy and healthy. My parents love me. God has given me many gifts. I can do anything I want to if I make a plan, concentrate and work toward it every day.

# Make yourself better today than yesterday.

Some of the happiest people are those who use their gifts to achieve the most they can. They don't waste anything that God gives them.

Every day is an opportunity to improve at something. Will you become a better reader today? What about practicing a sport or musical instrument?

Maybe you will use today to work on being a better sister, brother or child. You can be just a little nicer, or not get mad if things don't go your way. Maybe you could complete a responsibility without being asked or told.

All those things will make you better. If you don't get better at something today, you will have wasted a small part of your life that you can never get back.

I am smart, happy and healthy. My parents love me. God has given me many gifts. I can do anything I want to if I make a plan, concentrate and work toward it every day.

# *July 4th*

Independence Day

# Three very powerful words are
# "and then some."

It's good to carry out your responsibilities.
If you don't, that means someone else has
to take care of you.

But if you want to do something great in life,
you must do more than your responsibilities.
You have to do everything you are supposed
to do, *and then some.*

It is the extra that you do—the *and then
some*—that's the difference between being
just average and being able to do anything
you want to in life.

I am smart, happy and healthy. My parents
love me. God has given me many gifts. I can do
anything I want to if I make a plan, concentrate
and work toward it every day.

# Don't ever give up.

Everyone has things that don't work out the way they hope. When that happens, they have two choices. They can keep trying, working hard to get what they want.

Or they can quit.

If you keep trying there is no guarantee that you will achieve your goal. You might not.

But if you quit it is certain that you won't achieve your goal.

Many great things were done by people who failed and failed and failed before they finally achieved their goal.

Don't give up. If your goal is a good one, keep working at it until you reach it.

I am smart, happy and healthy. My parents love me. God has given me many gifts. I can do anything I want to if I make a plan, concentrate and work toward it every day.

# July 6th

## The happiest people

are usually the busiest people.

Have you ever noticed that a bad afternoon is one where you think you have nothing to do? "Mom... Dad... I'm bored. There's nothing to do."

That's not any fun, is it?

It's that way when you are a kid. It will be that way the rest of your life.

The happiest people are the ones who are busy doing important things.

I am smart, happy and healthy. My parents love me. God has given me many gifts. I can do anything I want to if I make a plan, concentrate and work toward it every day.

There is one guaranteed way
to end every argument.

# Be quiet.

When two people argue over something, they usually lose
their logic pretty quickly. They get caught up in emotions
and can't focus on whatever caused the disagreement.

So if you've forgotten what you're arguing about, why
continue arguing? Why not just be quiet?

It will confuse the other person and it will
create a lot less stress for you!

I am smart, happy and healthy. My parents
love me. God has given me many gifts. I can do
anything I want to if I make a plan, concentrate
and work toward it every day.

*July 8th*

# When you meet someone new,

spend the first 60 seconds
making the other person feel good.

---

When most people meet someone new, they
just talk about themselves, what they like to do,
the places they've been or the things they have.
They try to make themselves look good.

Instead of talking about yourself, focus on the
other person. Ask about where they live, what
they like to do or where they go to school.
Notice what they are wearing or try to learn
something unusual about them.

Remember this 60-second rule.

I am smart, happy and healthy. My parents
love me. God has given me many gifts. I can do
anything I want to if I make a plan, concentrate
and work toward it every day.

# Yelling usually doesn't help.

If you are in some kind of danger, let someone know. Yell. Scream. Blow a whistle. Throw a bag of popcorn in the air.

But yelling usually doesn't do anything except make people stop listening to you.

If you and someone are disagreeing about something, they will quit listening to you the moment you start yelling.

Other people will hear you very clearly if you yell, but the outcome won't be good. Try yelling at your parents some time and see what happens.

It's not a good way to get what you want, unless you want to get into trouble.

I am smart, happy and healthy. My parents love me. God has given me many gifts. I can do anything I want to if I make a plan, concentrate and work toward it every day.

If you are going to do something,

# work to be good at it.

As far as anyone knows, you only get to live on earth once. This isn't practice for the next time you are born in a hospital and go to elementary school.

So why not do the best you can this time?

It is so much more fun when you do your best at whatever you are doing. This is true at school, when you are playing, doing an art project, learning a musical instrument or playing a sport. If you are going to do something, do it well.

I am smart, happy and healthy. My parents love me. God has given me many gifts. I can do anything I want to if I make a plan, concentrate and work toward it every day.

# Your happiness depends on what you think.

There are two types of people in the world: those who are usually happy and those who usually aren't.

Many happy people have lives that look very similar to the lives of some of the unhappy people. Many of the unhappy people have lives that most people would consider great. What's the difference?

The way they think about their lives and react to the things that happen to them.

There are lots of things that happen in our lives. We can't control many of those. The great news, however, is that we do get to control what we think about. Therefore, we get to control whether or not we are happy.

I am smart, happy and healthy. My parents love me. God has given me many gifts. I can do anything I want to if I make a plan, concentrate and work toward it every day.

# Sadness is like weeds.

It grows where you don't take care of the good grass.

Look around a field. Where you mow it, the grass is soft and clean. There aren't many weeds. The briars are gone. So is the poison ivy.

When you plant and take care of your good grass, it pushes away all of the bad stuff—the weeds.

If you don't keep working on the good grass, however, the weeds will take over the field.

Happiness is good grass. It happens when we take care of our fields and work to get rid of the weeds.

I am smart, happy and healthy. My parents love me. God has given me many gifts. I can do anything I want to if I make a plan, concentrate and work toward it every day.

The best time to

# try something
# hard or new

is right after you succeed at something else.

Success is like a magnet, so use the power of that magnet to get more of it. When you have just won a game, scored 100 on a test or done something else that is great, that's the best time to try something new.

When something good happens, your mind is in a positive state and you can think better. Use that "success magnet" to bring more good things into your life.

I am smart, happy and healthy. My parents love me. God has given me many gifts. I can do anything I want to if I make a plan, concentrate and work toward it every day.

## July 14th

Alvin J. Fellows patents
the modern tape measure
1868

# If it's important, measure it.

There is a reason teachers grade your tests; it is important to know if you are learning what you are supposed to.

The teachers have to measure what you know.

Is there something important to you? When you make your plan, be sure to measure whether you're accomplishing your plan.

"I will hit 100 golf balls onto the green from the driving range each Saturday."

"I will do 20 minutes of stretching, followed by 10 back handsprings each day."

Don't just tell yourself that you want to do more back handsprings or hit more golf balls. Measure your goals.

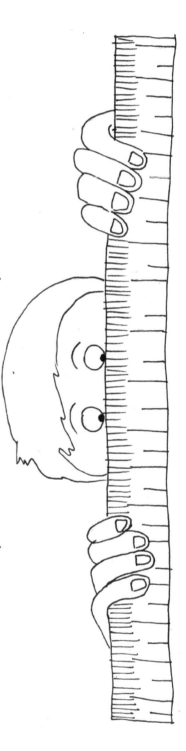

I am smart, happy and healthy. My parents love me. God has given me many gifts. I can do anything I want to if I make a plan, concentrate and work toward it every day.

# The "golden rule"

is a guide for you, not other people.

When Jesus said that people should treat others like they want to be treated, he didn't say we should only act that way if the other person is nice.

He didn't say that we should treat other people like they treat us.

We should be honest and truthful with everyone, not just the people we like or those who are nice to us.

When we treat someone with respect, we are actually treating ourselves with respect, too. Any time we are disrespectful to someone, it hurts that person—and it hurts our own soul too.

I am smart, happy and healthy. My parents love me. God has given me many gifts. I can do anything I want to if I make a plan, concentrate and work toward it every day.

# July 16th

Birthday of Sir Hugh Beaver
Founder of the Guinness Book of World Records
1890

What goal would you set if you knew it was

# impossible to fail?

Sometimes we don't set high goals for ourselves because we're afraid we might not meet them. Maybe we think other people should do those wonderful (or silly) things, like make straight A's, become president or be in the Guinness Book of World Records.

People who do those things, however, set goals—and then achieve them. They are just like you.

Set huge goals. You really can do anything you want to if you work at it the right way.

I CAN FLY!

I am smart, happy and healthy. My parents love me. God has given me many gifts. I can do anything I want to if I make a plan, concentrate and work toward it every day.

# Gossip hurts everyone.

Any time you say something about someone that you wouldn't say directly to them, you are gossiping. If you talk badly about people behind their backs you aren't helping anyone. That's a good enough reason not to do it. You should only do things that help people.

There are lots of other reasons not to gossip. Would you want people saying bad things about you? Even if something hurtful is true, there is no reason to repeat it.

If you wouldn't say it in front of the person, don't say it about them.

I am smart, happy and healthy. My parents love me. God has given me many gifts. I can do anything I want to if I make a plan, concentrate and work toward it every day.

# July 18th

# Worrying

is a lot like slapping yourself in the face over and over again; it's stupid and hurts until you stop doing it.

There is a difference between worrying about something and thinking about it. If you have a problem and are trying to solve it, that's a good thing. That's planning. That's using your brain.

But if you have a problem and are just sitting around depressed about it, you aren't doing anything to make the situation better. You are actually making it worse, because you are spending your energy on negative thoughts.

Quit worrying. When you have a problem, decide whether or not you can do anything to fix it. If you can, then fix it.

If you can't do anything about it, quit thinking about it. Work on things you can fix, and ignore the rest.

I am smart, happy and healthy. My parents love me. God has given me many gifts. I can do anything I want to if I make a plan, concentrate and work toward it every day.

# The mind is a muscle.

If you exercise it, it will get stronger.

If you don't, it will get smaller and weaker.

If you want your arms or shoulders to be big and strong, you will work out every day. You will lift weights, do push-ups and things like that. The harder we push ourselves, the stronger we become.

Your brain works the same way.

You go to school each day for seven hours. You sleep about eight or nine hours. That leaves eight free hours in the day. What do you do during that time? Do you read? Or do you only do lazy things with your mind, like watch television or play computer games?

If you want to have a strong mind when you are in high school or college or as an adult, you need to be doing "mind exercises" now.

I am smart, happy and healthy. My parents love me. God has given me many gifts. I can do anything I want to if I make a plan, concentrate and work toward it every day.

## July 20th

Birthday of Sir Edmund Hillary
First man known to climb Mt. Everest
1919

# Even a long trip starts with one step.

Sometimes when we look at a big project or task, it can seem huge. It might seem so huge that it almost seems impossible to do.

It doesn't matter, however, whether a task is large or small. Every task can be broken into small parts.

It's just like a trip. Even if you are going to take a long trip, you have to take the first step.

And the length of that step is the same whether the trip is up the stairs in your house or up the highest mountain in the world.

I am smart, happy and healthy. My parents love me. God has given me many gifts. I can do anything I want to if I make a plan, concentrate and work toward it every day.

# A major cause of unhappiness

is wandering around with no plans or goals.

People are happiest when they are moving in the direction of the things that are most important to them.

Do you really want to be a rock star? Then practicing music will make you happy. Do you want to be a great basketball player? Then you will want to do all the hard work it takes to get there.

But if you don't know what your goals are, you are probably just wandering around through your days. You have no plan, no purpose and no passion. That causes unhappiness.

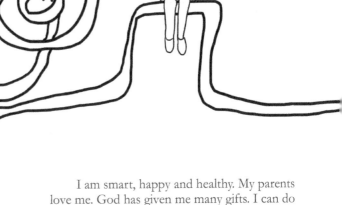

I am smart, happy and healthy. My parents love me. God has given me many gifts. I can do anything I want to if I make a plan, concentrate and work toward it every day.

# When we give more we get more.

When you are a child, your parents do everything for you. They feed you. They put you to bed. They help you learn to walk and talk. They change your dirty diapers.

That's not how life works when you get older.

As you get older, you will probably want more than just a bottle of milk and a clean diaper. You will want a house. You might want a car. Hopefully you will want a job. You will certainly want happy, loving relationships. None of those things happen unless you are first willing to give.

If you want a job, you must be willing to work. If you want a better job, you must be willing to work harder, smarter and better.

If you want close, loving friends, you must be a loving, giving friend, willing to do almost anything to help those you love.

I MADE CUPCAKES FOR THE WHOLE CLASS!

I am smart, happy and healthy. My parents love me. God has given me many gifts. I can do anything I want to if I make a plan, concentrate and work toward it every day.

# Be willing to change

when the situation changes.

A football team and its coaches work hard to decide what plays to run against the other team. They study the other team and practice. Sometimes, however, the quarterback gets ready to start the play and realizes that he needs to change the play.

This is called an audible. Maybe the play the team is about to run is going to fail. Maybe the quarterback sees a better opportunity.

Sometimes in life we need to audible.

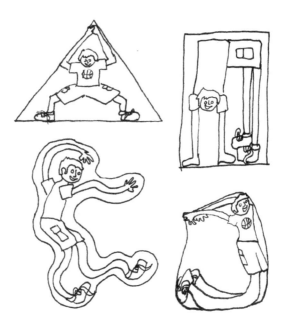

I am smart, happy and healthy. My parents love me. God has given me many gifts. I can do anything I want to if I make a plan, concentrate and work toward it every day.

# If you can change your thinking,

you can change anything.

You can change your thinking, but it's hard.
Maybe you have always thought you are an
average student. It is hard to think that you can
be a great student. You have to think you can be a
great student if you want to be one. The first step
in becoming a great student is deciding to be one.

The first step to any change occurs in your mind.
Change your thinking. You will be surprised
what can change after that.

I am smart, happy and healthy. My parents
love me. God has given me many gifts. I can do
anything I want to if I make a plan, concentrate
and work toward it every day.

# You will be happiest

doing things, not having things.

Some people think that they'll be happy if they have certain things. Maybe if they get a new outfit, or a fancy car or a house in a popular neighborhood they'll be happy.

Wrong. Things don't make people happy.

We become happy when we do things...when we do happy things. We become happiest when we do those things with other happy people.

Happiness happens when we collect great experiences, not when we collect fancy stuff.

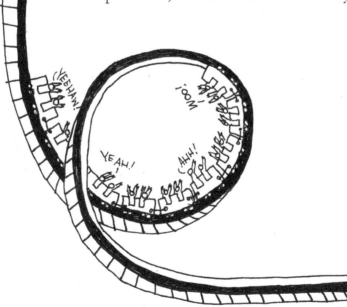

I am smart, happy and healthy. My parents love me. God has given me many gifts. I can do anything I want to if I make a plan, concentrate and work toward it every day.

# You are part of nature,

### not its owner.

Look around you; nature is full of trees, flowers, animals. The mountains are beautiful; so are the beaches, valleys and desert.

Like the blooming flowers in the spring, you are a part of the picture that makes nature beautiful.

You are not the artist; God is.

That doesn't mean that you can't plant flowers or help make the area around you more beautiful. But you do not have the right to destroy it. Nature is not your creation; it is your home.

I am smart, happy and healthy. My parents love me. God has given me many gifts. I can do anything I want to if I make a plan, concentrate and work toward it every day.

When we are hurting

# we are growing.

There are several ways to handle situations that are painful in our lives. We can try to ignore them by pretending that they don't exist. If you make a bad grade or your parents say something that hurts your feelings, what should you do?

Pretend it never happened?

No.

Try to figure out why it happened and if you did anything to cause it. It will hurt to think about it, but that is the only way you will get better. The pain tells you that you are getting stronger and can handle even harder struggles in the future.

I am smart, happy and healthy. My parents love me. God has given me many gifts. I can do anything I want to if I make a plan, concentrate and work toward it every day.

*July 28th*

# You won't regret starting early.

Some people get up early in the morning, happy and ready to do their work for the day. Other people try to stay in bed as long as possible, hoping an extra 15 minutes' sleep will make their day better.

Most people who get up early in the morning are successful at what they do.

You will be too.

There are lots of reasons for this. You won't be rushed or hurried. You will have time to think about your day or review your homework. You might have time for a little bit of reading or something else to make you a better person.

I am smart, happy and healthy. My parents love me. God has given me many gifts. I can do anything I want to if I make a plan, concentrate and work toward it every day.

# Never get mad at a dog for barking.

Dogs bark. That's what they do. Babies cry. Sometimes it rains. And your favorite team doesn't win all its games.

That's life, and you can't do anything about it.

When you get mad at a dog for barking, you're asking it to be something different from a dog. There is nothing wrong with the dog. There is something wrong with you. You're expecting something from someone (or something) that it does not do. You are expecting a dog to act like a human.

You are the one with the problem, not the dog.

When you expect someone to change from who they are to what they aren't, you are being weird. It's like expecting a dog not to bark.

I am smart, happy and healthy. My parents love me. God has given me many gifts. I can do anything I want to if I make a plan, concentrate and work toward it every day.

# July 30th

Birthday of Henry Ford
Founder of the Ford Motor Company
1863

# Your life is a car–and you are the driver.

Some day you will get a driver's license and begin to drive a car. At first your parents might not let you drive everywhere. They will give you some restrictions.

As you get older you will have fewer restrictions until you are an adult and can drive anywhere you want to. At that point you are completely in charge.

Everything you have done until then helped prepare you

for the day you became the adult driver. That's the way your life is.

Everything you are doing today is getting you ready for when you are the driver.

I am smart, happy and healthy. My parents love me. God has given me many gifts. I can do anything I want to if I make a plan, concentrate and work toward it every day.

You never see a goose flying with a flock of pigs.
In the wild, animals tend to run with animals that
are most like them, or they run with animals that can
teach them skills they need. People are the same way.

If you run around with someone, there is a
good chance you will become like them.

This is true whether the person is good or bad.
Their habits will likely become your habits—so

# pick friends who
# have great habits.

If you want to fly, don't hang around pigs.

I am smart, happy and healthy. My parents
love me. God has given me many gifts. I can do
anything I want to if I make a plan, concentrate
and work toward it every day.

# August 1st

Don't wait until you're ready.

# You're ready now.

Some people are talkers. All they do is talk about what they are going to do.

Other people are planners. They make detailed plans and lists of what they are going to do. As soon as the conditions are right and they have enough information or money or whatever, they say this will put their plan into action. They just keep waiting until they think the situation is perfect before they launch their plan.

Guess what? Things are never perfect. If you start sooner you might make more mistakes, but you will learn more and you will learn it faster. When is the best time to start work on your goal?

Today, right now.

I'M READY!

I am smart, happy and healthy. My parents love me. God has given me many gifts. I can do anything I want to if I make a plan, concentrate and work toward it every day.

How hard should you try?

# Harder.

Most people want things in life to be easy.
They expect things to be given to them or
they give up the first time things get tough.

The people who are happiest and most successful
in life are the ones who don't give up. They
know that everything has a cost, and the cost
of a really great life is really hard work.

I am smart, happy and healthy. My parents
love me. God has given me many gifts. I can do
anything I want to if I make a plan, concentrate
and work toward it every day.

# What matters is what you have,

not what you don't have.

Some people have things that you don't have. They might have a swimming pool or a pet you want, like a turtle. You can either spend all your time and energy wishing you had all the cool stuff your friends have or you can enjoy the things you have.

There is nothing wrong with wanting new things. Make a plan and work for them. Decide what you're going to do to get those things—then do it. Then concentrate on your plan, not the stuff you don't have.

I am smart, happy and healthy. My parents love me. God has given me many gifts. I can do anything I want to if I make a plan, concentrate and work toward it every day.

# Have courage.

People who have succeeded at all sorts of things have many different kinds of backgrounds. Some are good at math; some are good at social studies. Some are musicians. Some are athletes. Some are short. Some are tall. Some are women. Some are men.

But they all have courage. They are all willing to take a risk. They aren't afraid to do the things they need to do to accomplish great things.

Very few people are willing to take these kinds of risks, but very few people are great successes either.

I am smart, happy and healthy. My parents love me. God has given me many gifts. I can do anything I want to if I make a plan, concentrate and work toward it every day.

# August 5th

People have the hardest time changing the only thing over which they have complete control: their mind.

People can change their surroundings, but only a little bit. You can move from one room to another, and that is a change. But someone else decorated the room.
Or other people are in the room and decide what is going on while you are there.

Or a tree could fall on the room while you are in there. You can't completely control what happens in the room, although it is easy to walk into it.

# Yet you, and only you, can control your mind

—and you get to control it completely.
It's hard, but it's where all good things begin.

I am smart, happy and healthy. My parents love me. God has given me many gifts. I can do anything I want to if I make a plan, concentrate and work toward it every day.

# Everyone gets to decide his or her own future.

Some people don't make plans or don't work on their plans every day. When things happen to these people, it is mostly out of their control. Other people, or luck, are deciding their future.

Although you can't control everything that happens to you, you can take charge of it. You can make your plans. You can decide whether to work on them each day or not.

Someone is going to control your future. Will it be others or will it be you?

I am smart, happy and healthy. My parents love me. God has given me many gifts. I can do anything I want to if I make a plan, concentrate and work toward it every day.

# You won't be happy without being good at something.

When you have to write a page on dinosaurs for homework, you can do it a couple of different ways.

You can fill up the page with the first information you find. You can write silly sentences like "Dinosaurs don't live in Tennessee." That's true, but that doesn't prove that you researched very much.

Or you can learn as much as you can about dinosaurs and try to write the best page any kid has ever written.

Some people try to take short cuts when they are eight years old. They are usually the same people who take short cuts when they are 18 years old and 38 years old.

I am smart, happy and healthy. My parents love me. God has given me many gifts. I can do anything I want to if I make a plan, concentrate and work toward it every day.

# Don't waste your thoughts.

Each day has 1,440 minutes. What if each thought takes one minute? If you sleep eight hours a day, at most you can have only 960 thoughts each day.

Every time you have a negative thought, you are taking away the opportunity to have a good one. You are wasting a thought. You are wasting a resource that you can never get back.

Negative thoughts attract negative outcomes. Positive thoughts attract positive outcomes.

Which do you want to attract?

I am smart, happy and healthy. My parents love me. God has given me many gifts. I can do anything I want to if I make a plan, concentrate and work toward it every day.

If you are special, so is everyone else.

# Do you think you are important?

Of course you are. You are a child of God. You were created in his image. You are special; you have gifts that were given to you by God. There are things that you can do that no one else on earth can do.

This is true of every person you meet.

Anything that has been created by God should be treated with great respect. You should be treated with respect, both by yourself and by other people.

That means that other people should be treated with respect—especially by you.

I am smart, happy and healthy. My parents love me. God has given me many gifts. I can do anything I want to if I make a plan, concentrate and work toward it every day.

# Don't say, "I'll try."

### Say, "I will."

When people are looking at a project or a task
and say they will try to do it, they are already giving
themselves an excuse in case they fail.

There is just a little difference between saying
"I'll try" and saying "I won't."

If you have something to do, just do it. You don't
even have to talk about it. Tell yourself that
you will do it, then do it.

I am smart, happy and healthy. My parents
love me. God has given me many gifts. I can do
anything I want to if I make a plan, concentrate
and work toward it every day.

# August 11th

# We can't change other people,

but we can change ourselves.

A four-year-old boy and girl were playing together when they began to argue. They disagreed about what game they should play next. The little girl said, "I don't want to be your friend anymore."

After more arguing, she gave in—sort of. She sounded like a lot of grown-ups when she said, "I'll be your friend if you do what I want you to."

It doesn't work that way, but even most adults don't realize that. No matter how much you want other people to change, you can't make them change. You can decide who your friends are, but you can't make your friends act like you want them to. You either have to accept them as they are or get new friends.

I am smart, happy and healthy. My parents love me. God has given me many gifts. I can do anything I want to if I make a plan, concentrate and work toward it every day.

What would you try if you knew

# God wanted you to succeed?

The best support you can have in your life is the power of God. The good news is that God wants you to be happy and successful at the things you do in life.

Since God is on your side, you should be willing to try anything you really want to do. Do not be afraid of failure. If the things you want are consistent with the will of God, you can succeed.

I am smart, happy and healthy. My parents love me. God has given me many gifts. I can do anything I want to if I make a plan, concentrate and work toward it every day.

# August 13th

Birthday of John Logie Baird
Inventor of the color television
1888

Focus.

When you are watching a television show, do you move your head around the room? Do you look at the television one second, then a chair, then the dog?

No, you watch the TV. You focus on the show.

Television isn't important, but real life is. If something in your life is important, focus on it. Concentrate on it. Don't let other things—like chairs or dogs—distract you.

I am smart, happy and healthy. My parents love me. God has given me many gifts. I can do anything I want to if I make a plan, concentrate and work toward it every day.

# Your attitude

is the most important thing you own.

What do you own? Some clothes, books and toys.
Maybe a computer, a guitar or piano.

Those are all things you could lose. If you didn't have
enough money you might not ever replace them.

Would you be sad? Maybe. Maybe not.

It depends on your attitude. Your attitude is in your mind.
No one can take your mind or attitude away from you.
Your attitude influences whether you are happy or sad. It
helps you study for a test or it makes your mind wander.

The great thing is that you get to decide what your attitude
is. You always have it with you. And if you don't like it,
you can change it.

I am smart, happy and healthy. My parents
love me. God has given me many gifts. I can do
anything I want to if I make a plan, concentrate
and work toward it every day.

# Only share your dreams with positive people.

Dreams are powerful things. They work on our mind even when we are asleep. If we choose the right dreams, our mind will always be pulling us in the right direction.

It is also important to choose the right friends. We should want friends who pull us in the right direction, too.
If you tell your dream to people who don't pull you in the right direction, they will pull you away from that dream.

Dreams are very special.
Only share them with special people.

I am smart, happy and healthy. My parents love me. God has given me many gifts. I can do anything I want to if I make a plan, concentrate and work toward it every day.

# Be dependable.

How does it make you feel when someone tells you they are going to do something, then they don't do it? Not very good, does it? What if they say they are going to be somewhere at a certain time, and they are late or don't show up at all? It makes it hard to believe anything that person says.

If you are dependable, it means that people can believe what you say. It means that when you say you will do something, people know that you will do it.

Always be dependable. It is a great gift you can give others—and yourself.

I am smart, happy and healthy. My parents love me. God has given me many gifts. I can do anything I want to if I make a plan, concentrate and work toward it every day.

# Don't worry about problems

that haven't happened.

What were you worried about one year ago today?
What about a month ago or a week ago?
Do you remember? Probably not.

Most of the things we worry about never happen.
Maybe you worry about a monster sneaking into your
house and eating you. Guess what? There is no monster.
You wasted all that time and energy worrying.

There are some things you do need to worry about.
When real problems happen you need to do something
to help the situation. But it doesn't make sense to worry
about a problem that hasn't happened.

I am smart, happy and healthy. My parents
love me. God has given me many gifts. I can do
anything I want to if I make a plan, concentrate
and work toward it every day.

YOU DON'T
EVEN
EXIST!

# When you are doing something,

do that and nothing else.

The power of the mind is huge, but it must be focused. If your mind is trying to think of 30 things at the same time, it won't do a very good job at any of them.

The mind can only do one or two things really well at once.

When you are doing something important, put all of your mind's energy in that thing. If you are reading a book, block out all other noises and distractions. If you are hitting a tennis ball, focus on the ball. See the ball hit your racquet.

When you are praying, clear your mind of everything so you can hear God's wisdom.

Like anything else in life, concentration is a skill. You can learn it. You can practice it and get better at it.

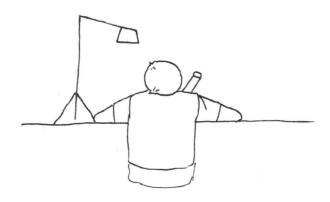

I am smart, happy and healthy. My parents love me. God has given me many gifts. I can do anything I want to if I make a plan, concentrate and work toward it every day.

# Anything is possible.

Imagine living more than 100 years ago, before the airplane was invented. What would people have said about someone with the idea that men could fly? They would have laughed at him. People did laugh at the Wright brothers—until they began to fly.

Who would have ever thought that you could get electricity from little holes in the wall? For thousands of years people would have never thought that you could fly to the moon.

In all of these examples, someone was willing to dream big. You should too.

I am smart, happy and healthy. My parents love me. God has given me many gifts. I can do anything I want to if I make a plan, concentrate and work toward it every day.

# Look for something good in other people.

When people meet you or are around you, they have a choice: they can look for the things that are good about you or they can look for your weaknesses.

Which do you hope they do?

You should do the same thing with other people.

Look for the good things in the people, especially when you first meet someone. Concentrate on those things. Maybe someone reads really well in class or they sing well. Maybe they have beautiful hair or they are very kind.

Notice those things.

SIEN HAS A BEAUTIFUL VOICE!

I am smart, happy and healthy. My parents love me. God has given me many gifts. I can do anything I want to if I make a plan, concentrate and work toward it every day.

# August 21st

One of the most dangerous phrases is "I'll do it later."

If you have something important to do,

## do it now. Don't wait.

You may have things you want to do before you get out of elementary or high school. Learn to play a musical instrument. Read a certain book. Write a book. Who knows? It could be anything.

Do it now. If you can't do it now, start it now. If you don't, you will wake up one morning—much sooner than you realize—and you will be out of school and it will be too late.

What are you waiting for?

I am smart, happy and healthy. My parents love me. God has given me many gifts. I can do anything I want to if I make a plan, concentrate and work toward it every day.

# If people trust you,

it gives you the chance to do more things in life.

Being dependable means always being honest. Do what you say you are going to do. That means you should always be on time. When you tell people you are going to do something they know they can believe it.

If people know that you will always do what you say you will do, they will trust you—and you will have the opportunity to do more important and exciting things in your life.

I am smart, happy and healthy. My parents love me. God has given me many gifts. I can do anything I want to if I make a plan, concentrate and work toward it every day.

# A negative mental attitude

attracts problems like a dead cat attracts flies.

When you see a dead animal on the road or in the woods,
there is almost always a bunch of flies around it.
Like problems in life, those flies are pests.

And like a dead animal in the middle of the road,
when you think negative thoughts you attract
flies—and problems—into your life.

Every day, we make a decision to prepare our minds to
attract and receive either problems or blessings. If we have
a bad attitude, we will attract more problems than blessings.

When you have a positive attitude,
you attract more blessings.

I am smart, happy and healthy. My parents
love me. God has given me many gifts. I can do
anything I want to if I make a plan, concentrate
and work toward it every day.

# Notice everything around you.

Too many people go through life paying attention only to the things right in front of them.

If you want to get the most enjoyment out of life, however, try to notice everything. See the plants and trees. See if you can hear things that you can't see. When you are in a new place, look around and really enjoy how many different new things there are.

Do the same thing when you are around new people.

Notice the small details.

I am smart, happy and healthy. My parents love me. God has given me many gifts. I can do anything I want to if I make a plan, concentrate and work toward it every day.

Other than your parents and God,

# no one can think you are worth more than you do.

You may have a lot of people who think you can do many things. Your teachers, family members and friends may all look up to you or have high expectations of you.

The most important thing is that you understand how valuable you are. You must see the value in yourself, because you are the one who decides what your true worth actually is.

I am smart, happy and healthy. My parents love me. God has given me many gifts. I can do anything I want to if I make a plan, concentrate and work toward it every day.

No one ever gets what they want
# by complaining or whining.

If there is something you want, make up your mind to get it.
Then do everything within your power to meet that goal.
If you always do that with a positive attitude, you
will increase your chance of success and happiness.

When you are mad or in a bad mood, you attract more
bad things into your life. You probably won't get
the thing you are hoping and planning for.

If things don't go your way, don't complain;
stay positive and see that good things happen.

YOU STILL
CAN'T HAVE IT,
BETHANY!

I am smart, happy and healthy. My parents
love me. God has given me many gifts. I can do
anything I want to if I make a plan, concentrate
and work toward it every day.

## *August 27th*

Birthday of Mother Teresa
Lifelong minister to the needy
1910

# Help someone today.

Every day someone does something to help you.
Sometimes it's a little thing, like opening the door for
you. Sometimes it's something you take for granted,
like driving you to school. Sometimes it's something
really big like helping you learn to sing a song or
do a back handspring.

How would your life be if those people didn't do
those things to help you?

When those people help you, not only is it good
for you, it's good for them. Everyone is blessed
when they help others.

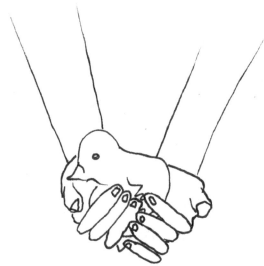

I am smart, happy and healthy. My parents
love me. God has given me many gifts. I can do
anything I want to if I make a plan, concentrate
and work toward it every day.

# Always do what you say you will do,

when you say you will do it.

It's easy to say you will do something. Promises are easy. "Yes ma'am, I will do that." "Yes sir, I will be there at seven o'clock."

Will you actually DO what you say? Too many people don't.

Many people think that it's good enough to *almost* or *usually* do what they say they're going to do.

If another person doesn't always do what they say, how will you know when to believe them?

The same is true for you. If you don't always do what you say, how will people know when to believe you?

I am smart, happy and healthy. My parents love me. God has given me many gifts. I can do anything I want to if I make a plan, concentrate and work toward it every day.

# Much of what you will want

in life depends on the
cooperation of others.

Don't live your life trying to please others.
You should only try to please yourself. That doesn't
mean, however, that you don't need other people.
You do need other people.

There are very few things you can do in life that
don't need help from one or more people. If you
can't get along with other people, you will be limited
in the things you can accomplish and enjoy.

I am smart, happy and healthy. My parents
love me. God has given me many gifts. I can do
anything I want to if I make a plan, concentrate
and work toward it every day.

It's usually easy to tell the difference between

# right and wrong.

Every time you do something, you have
a choice: you can do something that is good
or bad. Sometimes when we do things that
we wish we hadn't, we're tempted to say,
"I didn't know that was wrong."

That usually isn't true.

God has given us the ability
to tell right from wrong.
It is almost always easy to tell the
difference, if we will just stop and think.

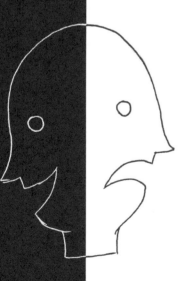

I am smart, happy and healthy. My parents
love me. God has given me many gifts. I can do
anything I want to if I make a plan, concentrate
and work toward it every day.

# Pick good role models.

A role model is someone you respect and hope to be like.
They make good decisions and give good advice.
Often, it is someone older than you.

You probably have one or more role models already, even
if you've never thought about it.

People usually become like the folks they respect and
admire. Make sure you respect really good people.

I am smart, happy and healthy. My parents
love me. God has given me many gifts. I can do
anything I want to if I make a plan, concentrate
and work toward it every day.

# A tree rots from the inside out.

So do people.

Look at a tree that has been cut open and lying on the ground for a while. The inside can be rotted even though the outside still might look strong and healthy.

A person can be the same way.

If a person doesn't stay healthy and begins to rot, you won't notice it at first. It starts as little things, like not thinking good thoughts or maybe being sick a lot.

The problems begin on the inside.

If a person is rotting on the inside, sooner or later they will fall—just like a mighty tree.

I am smart, happy and healthy. My parents love me. God has given me many gifts. I can do anything I want to if I make a plan, concentrate and work toward it every day.

*September 2nd*

# It takes two people to fight.

Have you ever seen anyone fight by herself?
Have you ever heard anybody arguing with himself?

That would look pretty stupid or silly, wouldn't it?

Don't ever blame a fight or argument on someone else.
If you are arguing or fighting with someone, that's a
decision you made. It's not the other person's fault.

I am smart, happy and healthy. My parents
love me. God has given me many gifts. I can do
anything I want to if I make a plan, concentrate
and work toward it every day.

# Try new things.

If you always do the same things, you will always get the same things. The only way to have new experiences is to try new things.

Try new foods. When you get the chance, meet new people. Try new sports. Read a book you think might be weird. Who knows? You might love it. You might even find something you want to do for the rest of your life.

Life is a collection of experiences. Try to collect a new one every day.

THAT ONE WAS FUN!

I am smart, happy and healthy. My parents love me. God has given me many gifts. I can do anything I want to if I make a plan, concentrate and work toward it every day.

# Get along with others.

The people who do more and are happiest in life are the ones who can see things from the other guy's point of view. They don't fight.

They work with other people, not against them.

I am smart, happy and healthy. My parents love me. God has given me many gifts. I can do anything I want to if I make a plan, concentrate and work toward it every day.

# What do you think about the most?

That is what you will probably be good at.

No matter what we do in life, we will run into problems. Everyone has times when things don't go their way. Successful people are the ones who run into problems, then try even harder. They don't get frustrated.

It is easiest to work at something if you have a strong passion for it. Do you think about it all the time? If so, you are more likely to handle temporary setbacks.

I am smart, happy and healthy. My parents love me. God has given me many gifts. I can do anything I want to if I make a plan, concentrate and work toward it every day.

# You don't get stronger pushing a wagon downhill.

When a child is about one year old, he is strong enough to lift a small bottle of ketchup. Then he tries to lift something heavier—but he can't. He isn't strong enough. But he keeps trying. Every time he tries and fails, his muscles get stronger.

That happens his entire life. Every time he tries to do something that is hard, he gets stronger and becomes a better person.

If he only lifted feathers he would never get stronger.

If we never did hard things in our lives, life would be pretty easy—but we would never be strong enough to lift even a bottle of ketchup.

WHY AREN'T MY MUSCLES GETTING BIGGER?

I am smart, happy and healthy. My parents love me. God has given me many gifts. I can do anything I want to if I make a plan, concentrate and work toward it every day.

# In order to be happy or successful,

you must know what you want.

Be clear about it. Know exactly what it is.

When you know the thing or things that are important to you, you will know the thing or things at which you are most likely to be good at.

I WANT TO DO A TOE TOUCH!

I am smart, happy and healthy. My parents love me. God has given me many gifts. I can do anything I want to if I make a plan, concentrate and work toward it every day.

# Compliment other people.

A couple of things happen when you tell someone something nice about themselves. First, it makes the other person feel good. Everyone loves to hear something good about themselves.

It will also make you feel good. Often we think we have to say good things about ourselves to make us feel good. But if we say something nice about someone else, it actually makes us feel better than if we say it about ourselves.

When you compliment someone else, it makes two people feel like winners!

I am smart, happy and healthy. My parents love me. God has given me many gifts. I can do anything I want to if I make a plan, concentrate and work toward it every day.

Birthday of Harland David Sanders
(aka Colonel Sanders)
Founder of Kentucky Fried Chicken
1890

# If you were a fish,

would you go to the ocean on vacation?

One of the great joys in life is experiencing new things. How boring would it be to eat fried chicken every night for dinner? Pretty boring.

Imagine if you sat in the same room your entire life, or never met any new people.

One way to bring great fun into your life is to experience new things. Take advantage of new opportunities.

I am smart, happy and healthy. My parents love me. God has given me many gifts. I can do anything I want to if I make a plan, concentrate and work toward it every day.

WELL, THIS
ISN'T MUCH FUN.

# The world needs followers.

Let it be someone else.

The easiest thing in the world is to let someone else make your decisions. Going where the crowd wants to go. Always doing the things your friends want to do. Wearing the same clothes that everyone else wants to wear.

When you get into this habit about the small things, you will probably fall into this habit about the big things, too. In school, there will be groups of people who do drugs and groups who do not. Who is the person who decides for the group if they will do drugs or not? The leader.

Who is the person who decides for a group what games to play at recess or whether or not to take their grades seriously? The leader.

If you are a leader, you will not only help yourself but you will help the large number of people who choose to be followers.

I am smart, happy and healthy. My parents love me. God has given me many gifts. I can do anything I want to if I make a plan, concentrate and work toward it every day.

# Try to have your best dreams

when you are awake.

When you are asleep and dream, you don't get to decide what the dream is about. You don't get to decide who is in the dream or how it ends. It might be a scary dream, a sad one or a happy one.

You can also dream during the day. When you do, you get to decide what happens. You can dream about wonderful things you want to do. You can dream about places you want to go or people you want to meet. In these daydreams, anything is possible.

You may even find your goals in these daydreams.

AM I DREAMING OR AM I IN FIRST PLACE??

I am smart, happy and healthy. My parents love me. God has given me many gifts. I can do anything I want to if I make a plan, concentrate and work toward it every day.

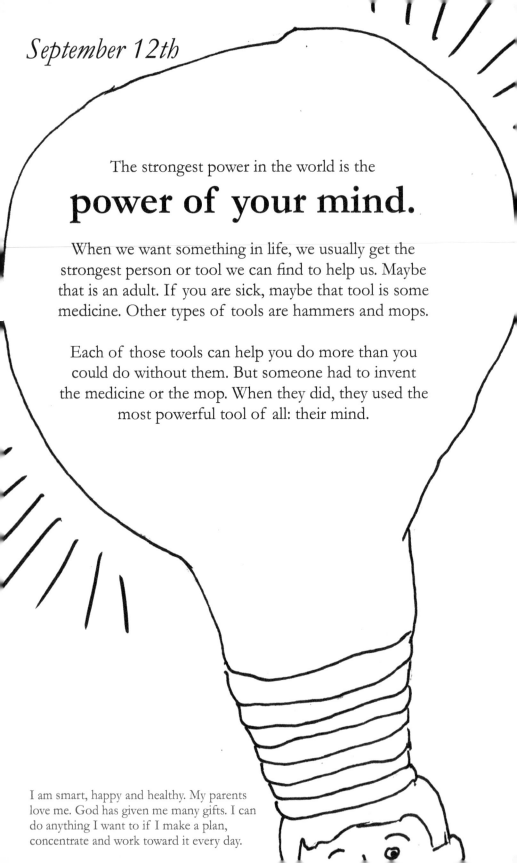

*September 12th*

The strongest power in the world is the

# power of your mind.

When we want something in life, we usually get the strongest person or tool we can find to help us. Maybe that is an adult. If you are sick, maybe that tool is some medicine. Other types of tools are hammers and mops.

Each of those tools can help you do more than you could do without them. But someone had to invent the medicine or the mop. When they did, they used the most powerful tool of all: their mind.

I am smart, happy and healthy. My parents love me. God has given me many gifts. I can do anything I want to if I make a plan, concentrate and work toward it every day.

# There is a reason they put sugar in candy.

If a fly smells sugar or something sweet, it will go to that sweet smell and see what there is to eat.

People are the same way. They want to be around things and other people who are sweet and pleasant, not mean and bitter.

If you want someone to be nice to you, be nice to them first. It's magic that almost always works.

I am smart, happy and healthy. My parents love me. God has given me many gifts. I can do anything I want to if I make a plan, concentrate and work toward it every day.

# There are some things you can control

and some things you can't.

Don't worry about the things you can't.

You are responsible for everything you do in life, but many of the things in your life are outside your control.

All you can do is control how you react to them.

Don't get upset when it rains; there is nothing you can do to keep it from raining. However, if the weatherman tells you that it is probably going to rain today, don't plan to mow the grass. Instead, plan to do something inside. Or do something outside you don't mind doing in the rain.

If you get upset about things you can't control, you will spend much of your life getting upset.

I am smart, happy and healthy. My parents love me. God has given me many gifts. I can do anything I want to if I make a plan, concentrate and work toward it every day.

# If you tell yourself

something enough times, your mind will
believe it—even if it isn't true.

A part of your mind is working all the time, even when
you don't realize it. It's called your subconscious. This is
like the background music of your life. It is
always playing. You hear it whether you notice it or not.

This part of your mind will believe whatever you tell it,
especially if you tell it over and over again. If you tell
your background mind that you are ugly, stupid or a
goofball, your mind will believe it and start
making you act like that.

But if you tell your mind that you are beautiful,
handsome, smart and healthy, your mind will
help you become those things, too.

I'M A KING!

I am smart, happy and healthy. My parents
love me. God has given me many gifts. I can do
anything I want to if I make a plan, concentrate
and work toward it every day.

*September 16th*

Birthday of David Cutcliffe
American football coach
1954

# Wherever you go,

leave it better than you found it.

When Coach Cutcliffe was a young boy, his family was about to leave a park after a day of games and picnics. It was almost dark; they were the last ones to leave.

David's father stopped his kids from loading the car. "I want you to go through this park and pick up every piece of trash," he told them. The children objected. They hadn't left any garbage in the park.

Mr. Cutcliffe knew that, but didn't care.

When they were finished, the kids were proud of the spotless park. They were leaving it better than they found it. They were leaving the park cleaner than it was when they arrived.

I am smart, happy and healthy. My parents love me. God has given me many gifts. I can do anything I want to if I make a plan, concentrate and work toward it every day.

*California Here we come!*

By themselves,
# plans are not worth anything.

Before you go on a trip, it is good to know where you are going. You decide what roads to take, when to leave and when you expect to arrive at your destination.

If you never get in the car and go, however, the plans are worthless.

Plans are important. They are extremely important. But that is all some people do. They plan and plan and plan. They never *do*.

It is good to be a planner. It is much more important to be a *doer*.

I am smart, happy and healthy. My parents love me. God has given me many gifts. I can do anything I want to if I make a plan, concentrate and work toward it every day.

# Your education

doesn't really begin until you get out of school.

For 13 years you go to elementary, middle and high school. Then you go to college. Then maybe you go to school some more.

Then it is time to start really learning.

The people who succeed in life are the ones who use those first 17 years of school as a long lesson in *how to learn*. After that, they use every day as an opportunity to learn something about their career or something else that is very important to them.

The people who stop learning when they are 22 years old are the ones who very quickly stop growing in every area of their lives.

Never stop learning.

I am smart, happy and healthy. My parents love me. God has given me many gifts. I can do anything I want to if I make a plan, concentrate and work toward it every day.

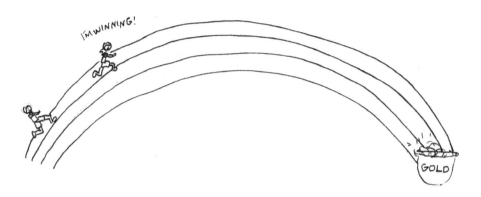

# It is a long walk

to the pot of gold at the end of the rainbow.

Everyone wants good things in life, but good things come with a price. They are not handed to us. We have to go get them.

Most of the best things in life require work. Really hard work. Successful people work until they sweat and often until it hurts. But they know that the short-term pain will result in great things in the long term.

Do not be afraid of pain. When you work so hard that you don't think you can work anymore, you are probably wrong. There is probably more that you can do—and as a result, more good things that will happen to you.

I am smart, happy and healthy. My parents love me. God has given me many gifts. I can do anything I want to if I make a plan, concentrate and work toward it every day.

# Don't treat your body

worse than you do your dog.

If you love your dog, you feed it well. You make sure
it gets enough exercise. You don't abuse it. You give it
clean water every day. You realize that if the dog dies
you can always get another one, but you can't really
replace a living thing. You are the same way.
Be sure you treat yourself the same way.

You do not get another *you*. Treat yourself well.
Exercise. Eat the right things. Get plenty of rest,
and plenty of activity.

You cannot be replaced.

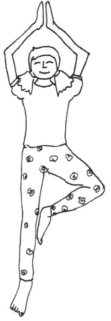

I am smart, happy and healthy. My parents
love me. God has given me many gifts. I can do
anything I want to if I make a plan, concentrate
and work toward it every day.

# Don't keep making the same mistakes.

Mistakes are a part of life. Everyone makes them, including parents, teachers and kids. Successful people know that mistakes happen.

Successful people also try very hard not to make the same mistake twice.

A mistake is an opportunity to learn. If you make the same mistake twice, it means you didn't learn anything. And that means the mistake was a terrible waste of your time and energy.

I am smart, happy and healthy. My parents love me. God has given me many gifts. I can do anything I want to if I make a plan, concentrate and work toward it every day.

*September 22nd*

It's not an accident that

# some people are happier than others.

They decide to be.

Have you ever noticed that some people seem to be happier than other people? They smile more. They laugh more. They seem to enjoy more things in their life than other people.

Do you think there is something special about their life?

No. They have problems just like everyone else.

When bad things happen in their life, they don't forget about the good things that also happen in their life. They focus on the good, not the bad.

I am smart, happy and healthy. My parents love me. God has given me many gifts. I can do anything I want to if I make a plan, concentrate and work toward it every day.

# Be careful what you dream.

### It might come true.

If you have a good dream and you think about it every day, there is a chance that you may eventually get that dream.

So better make sure that you dream big!

Of course, you need to do more than just concentrate on your dream every day. You need a plan and you have to work toward it. But first you need a dream. Have a big one.

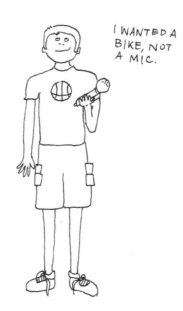

I WANTED A BIKE, NOT A MIC.

I am smart, happy and healthy. My parents love me. God has given me many gifts. I can do anything I want to if I make a plan, concentrate and work toward it every day.

# God is bigger than you think.

People can be smart. People invented electricity, computers and popcorn—all the really important things in life.

But no matter how smart we are, there's no way that we can understand the mysteries of life. Church is one place people try to do that. Prayer is one way to try to understand God's will in our life.

However, these are only tools. They are limited because we are limited. We are not God, although God is within each of us.

Is that complicated? Yes. It is so complicated that it is impossible to understand. It is one of the mysteries of life.

I am smart, happy and healthy. My parents love me. God has given me many gifts. I can do anything I want to if I make a plan, concentrate and work toward it every day.

# If you can imagine it, you can do it.

When you think of something, you are beginning to give it life. You get it started. If you have an idea, and you really believe in that idea, you can accomplish whatever that idea is.

This works for good things and bad things. If you get the idea that you are smart and are going to invent a flying car or become a doctor, you can do that. You really can.

If you get the idea that you are stupid or that you will live under a bridge someday, there is a good chance that will happen.

If you think it and believe it, it really might happen.

I am smart, happy and healthy. My parents love me. God has given me many gifts. I can do anything I want to if I make a plan, concentrate and work toward it every day.

DOCTOR BETHANY

# September 26th

Birthday of Johnny Appleseed
1774

# Plant a seed every day.

When you have a slice of a juicy tomato or a fresh ear of corn, how do you think that happens?

It takes several months of work for the farmer to produce those vegetables and bring them to the store so we can buy and enjoy them. It takes planning and patience.

Too many times in our lives, we want to do something today so we can enjoy it today. Imagine if we could only eat the things that we could plant and grow in one day. We would probably just eat a bunch of dirt.

The best things in life take some time. Always plan ahead. Every day, think about something that is important to you that will take time to accomplish. Do something today that will help you move in that direction. When you do, you're planting a seed.

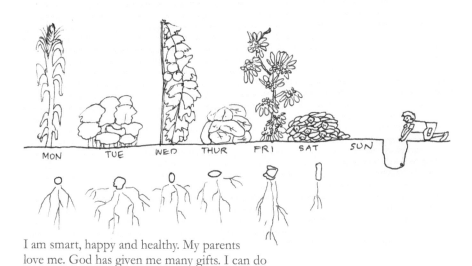

MON    TUE    WED    THUR    FRI    SAT    SUN

I am smart, happy and healthy. My parents love me. God has given me many gifts. I can do anything I want to if I make a plan, concentrate and work toward it every day.

# Quit hoping the other person will change.

"If my sister would just stop doing that, I would be happier." "If my parents would be more like this, then everything would be great." "My life would be so much better if my brother would just change."

Guess what? Most people don't change. If you are waiting for the other person to change, you are going to have a long wait.

So what should you do?

You have to learn to accept people as they are—because they are going to have to accept you as you are, too.

I am smart, happy and healthy. My parents love me. God has given me many gifts. I can do anything I want to if I make a plan, concentrate and work toward it every day.

## September 28th

The more you do something,

# the easier it gets.

This is true whether you are doing
a good thing or a bad thing.

If you get up early one morning and exercise, it's
easier to do it again the second day. It's easier to make
your bed after you've gotten in the habit of doing it.

If you tell someone a lie, it will be easier to tell
another lie the next day. If you are mean once,
you will find it easier to be mean again.

Be careful what you do, even if you think you
will only do it once. You probably won't.

I am smart, happy and healthy. My parents
love me. God has given me many gifts. I can do
anything I want to if I make a plan, concentrate
and work toward it every day.

# Concentrate.

Most people just go through life and never really think about what they want. Things happen to them and they either accept them or get mad about them.

They don't think about why things happen to them.

The more you think about something, the more likely it is to happen. Maybe you will come up with a great idea to help you do something you're thinking about.

What if you want to invent a flying car? That would be very tough, wouldn't it? If you thought about it all day, every day, it would probably still be hard.

However, imagine how hard it would be if you never thought about it. *It would be impossible.* The only way to do something hard is to concentrate on it.

I am smart, happy and healthy. My parents love me. God has given me many gifts. I can do anything I want to if I make a plan, concentrate and work toward it every day.

# Don't waste any energy

thinking or talking about negative things or people.

Remember that the mind is a powerful magnet that pulls things toward you. Your mind doesn't know if you're thinking about good things or bad things. It just knows that when you start thinking or talking about something, it will start pulling that thing toward you.

This powerful force is very dangerous if you aren't careful.

You only have 24 hours in a day. Don't waste any of them. When you spend any time talking about negative things or people, you've wasted some of your most valuable resources: your time and energy.

I am smart, happy and healthy. My parents love me. God has given me many gifts. I can do anything I want to if I make a plan, concentrate and work toward it every day.

# If you want more,

then you need to give or earn more.

At some time in your life, you will want
your parents to treat you more like an adult.
You will want to do things or go places
like teenagers. You will want to grow up.

If you are eight years old and want to do something
that you see 10-year-olds or 12-year-olds doing, then
you need to begin acting like a 10- or 12-year-old.
Don't wait. Do more than you are already doing, and
you will get more than you are already getting.

I am smart, happy and healthy. My parents
love me. God has given me many gifts. I can do
anything I want to if I make a plan, concentrate
and work toward it every day.

## October 2nd

If you want the things around you to change,

# try changing yourself.

Many times in our lives we wish things were different.
Maybe we wish our parents, friends or teachers
would treat us differently.

Maybe we wish we had different things, like a new
bicycle or dog. Or maybe we just wish it would snow.

Usually when we think that we would be happier
if something or someone around us would change,
it means that there is something wrong with
us—not the other people.

When you wish things were different,
always ask this question: "What can I be
doing to make the situation better?"

Start with yourself. That's where most
answers—and problems—are.

I am smart, happy and healthy. My parents
love me. God has given me many gifts. I can do
anything I want to if I make a plan, concentrate
and work toward it every day.

# Everyone wants things,

but for most people those are just wishes.

"I want a new bicycle." "I want to go to the beach."
Unless the person has a plan, those are just wishes.
It's like hoping the tooth fairy leaves a bicycle
or a beach under your pillow!

If you really want something, you have to be willing
to give something for it. Maybe you have to pay money
for a bicycle. Maybe the price you have to pay is hard
work if you want to make good grades or learn to
play a musical instrument.

Maybe you even have to help your parents more
around the house if you want to go on vacation.

Don't wish for things. Decide what you want. Then decide
what you have to give so you can have it.

Then do it.

I am smart, happy and healthy. My parents
love me. God has given me many gifts. I can do
anything I want to if I make a plan, concentrate
and work toward it every day.

# If you never get started,

you will never finish.

Whatever you want to do, you will never finish it unless you get started. It doesn't matter if the task is easy or hard. It doesn't matter if it is going to take a few minutes or a few weeks. The only way you have a chance to finish the task is to start working on it.

Do not wait. Get started.

I am smart, happy and healthy. My parents love me. God has given me many gifts. I can do anything I want to if I make a plan, concentrate and work toward it every day.

# Treat others

the way you would want
them to treat you.

Think about this all day today. What are
the things that you love people to do with you?
What do you like to hear people say? How do
other people make you feel good?

Those are the things you should be doing today.

Each day, you should do something to make
another person's day better.

What are you going to do that's good for another
person today? How are you going to help someone?

I am smart, happy and healthy. My parents
love me. God has given me many gifts. I can do
anything I want to if I make a plan, concentrate
and work toward it every day.

# Don't worry

about trying to get other people to like you.

Just be the best you can be. People will either like you or not. If you try too hard for attention, you will either dominate other people or make them dislike you.

You really can't make anyone do anything. All you can do is control yourself. If you change yourself to try to make someone like you, then you won't be yourself—and you probably won't like yourself.

If you don't like yourself, it's almost certain other people won't like you.

I'M AWESOME!

I am smart, happy and healthy. My parents love me. God has given me many gifts. I can do anything I want to if I make a plan, concentrate and work toward it every day.

There is a certain type of

# power in a group.

Two people working together on the same goal can do more than if each of them were working on the same goal by themselves.

The greatest accomplishments throughout the history of man happened when groups of people worked together to achieve a goal.

Henry Ford had a group of advisers who helped him succeed at building an automobile. Thomas Edison had a whole army of engineers and scientists helping him. Even Jesus had 12 apostles.

I am smart, happy and healthy. My parents love me. God has given me many gifts. I can do anything I want to if I make a plan, concentrate and work toward it every day.

What would happen

# if everyone did what you do?

You may think that some little thing you do doesn't matter. Maybe you are about to throw a piece of paper out the window. One piece of trash won't make much difference. But what if everyone did that? That would be a lot of trash.

Now think about making a good decision.

When you make a good decision, imagine if everyone did the same thing. What if everyone cleaned up after themselves? What if everyone tried to help their neighbor or family member? What if everyone tried just a little bit to make the world a better place?

That would be a lot of good.

I am smart, happy and healthy. My parents love me. God has given me many gifts. I can do anything I want to if I make a plan, concentrate and work toward it every day.

# Don't worry about them.

Worry about you.

Sometimes a friend or your brother or sister will do something you think they shouldn't. Maybe they didn't do their homework or you don't like the way they dress or the way they talk.

Before you can tell other people what they ought to be doing, you need to be doing everything perfectly yourself. Since you are never going to be perfect, you will always have enough of your own things to worry about that you won't need to criticize the other guy.

WHAT SHOULD I WEAR TODAY?

I am smart, happy and healthy. My parents love me. God has given me many gifts. I can do anything I want to if I make a plan, concentrate and work toward it every day.

# You are special.

When every person is born, God gives them certain gifts. Some people are very, very intelligent. Some people have a healthy body and mind. Others have a great sense of humor. Sometimes we can't see those gifts in others, but they are there.

If you use these gifts with a clear goal in mind and hard work, you can do anything you want to do with your life. Anything is possible because you are special.

I am smart, happy and healthy. My parents love me. God has given me many gifts. I can do anything I want to if I make a plan, concentrate and work toward it every day.

# Don't try to think

and talk at the same time.

There are many ways we learn things. Almost all of them have to do with listening. We listen to teachers. We listen to our parents. Sometimes we even learn when we listen to our friends or siblings.

We learn when we listen to our hearts. We learn when we listen to the wisdom we find in books and in our life experiences. We cannot listen when we are also talking. Some people talk, hoping they sound smart. But if you want to be smart, listen.

I am smart, happy and healthy. My parents love me. God has given me many gifts. I can do anything I want to if I make a plan, concentrate and work toward it every day.

*October 12th*

When something good happens to you,

# take time to enjoy it.

Be thankful for all of the blessings in your life.

One of the easy ways to show thanks for your blessings is to simply enjoy them. Be aware of the things that are happening in your life, and when something good is happening, slow down and enjoy it.

Thank God for it. Thank anyone in your life who helped make that moment possible.

Whether it is a great meal, a beautiful sunny afternoon, conversation with a great friend, or even time alone with a good book, take the time to enjoy the good things in your life.

I am smart, happy and healthy. My parents love me. God has given me many gifts. I can do anything I want to if I make a plan, concentrate and work toward it every day.

When something good happens to you,

# take time to learn from it.

You can learn from bad things that happen in life, but there are lessons when good things happen, too.

How did you make 100 on that difficult test? It wasn't an accident. You probably studied. When your team does well or you have a good music recital, ask yourself why that happened.

Then do it some more.

I am smart, happy and healthy. My parents love me. God has given me many gifts. I can do anything I want to if I make a plan, concentrate and work toward it every day.

# When something bad happens,

take time to learn from it.

Bad things are going to happen in your life.
There is nothing you can do to completely prevent it.

When bad things happen, you have a choice. You can
either get mad, sad and frustrated, or you can try to figure
out if you helped cause the bad thing to happen.

What if you make a 70 on a test? That certainly is a bad thing.
You could get mad and depressed and mope about it. Or you
could try to figure out why you did so poorly on the test. Did
you not study hard enough? Did you not pay attention in class?
Could you study differently?

Learn from the unpleasant things that happen in life.

I am smart, happy and healthy. My parents
love me. God has given me many gifts. I can do
anything I want to if I make a plan, concentrate
and work toward it every day.

# Don't be a dirt kicker.

Have you ever watched a baseball game and seen a pitcher kick the ground after a batter hits a home run? Or maybe a quarterback throws an interception, so he hangs his head as he walks off the field, then kicks the turf in anger?

Do you think kicking the dirt will keep them from throwing an interception or a bad pitch in the future? Of course not.

Most dirt kickers either can't control their emotions, or they are putting on a little show, trying to convince other people they are upset. Neither one of these is helpful. The best thing to do when something doesn't go your way is to try to figure out what you did wrong and what you can do better in the future. Think. Concentrate.

Don't pitch a fit. It won't help—and it will just mess up your shoes.

I am smart, happy and healthy. My parents love me. God has given me many gifts. I can do anything I want to if I make a plan, concentrate and work toward it every day.

# Make a decision

or other people will always be in charge of
what happens in your life.

Gather information. Then make a decision.
Don't wait until you know every piece of
information; you can never know everything.

Don't worry about making a mistake, because
sometimes you will. The only people who don't make
mistakes are the people who don't make decisions.

It is sad to see a person who can't decide little things, like
what to have for dinner or what clothes to wear. People
who have trouble making decisions about little things will
have trouble making decisions about big things.

I am smart, happy and healthy. My parents
love me. God has given me many gifts. I can do
anything I want to if I make a plan, concentrate
and work toward it every day.

It is impossible to understand exactly what God is. But God is not Santa Claus.

Try not to look at God as a place to go when you want stuff.

In the Bible, God let King Solomon have anything he wanted. Solomon could have had riches or power. He could probably even have asked God for a car, even though they hadn't been invented yet.

# What did he ask for?

One of the best things to ask for when you are in that quiet place seeking help is wisdom. Ask God to help you be wise enough to accept things when they don't go your way. And ask God for the wisdom to make good decisions so maybe things will go your way more often.

I am smart, happy and healthy. My parents love me. God has given me many gifts. I can do anything I want to if I make a plan, concentrate and work toward it every day.

# Everyone is on a team.

Choose good team members.

Do you think any great athlete ever won a basketball or football championship by himself? Of course not. Even a great player needs a good team around him if he wants a chance to win.

Life is the same way. And you get to choose many of your teammates.

Some of the people on your team have already been decided for you: your teachers and parents, for example.

You get to choose your other teammates: your friends and others you spend time with. These are the people who will help you win championships or will drag you into the losing column. Make sure you pick team members who will help you win.

I am smart, happy and healthy. My parents love me. God has given me many gifts. I can do anything I want to if I make a plan, concentrate and work toward it every day.

# Be careful

with the spirit you let be around you.

Everything that lives or has ever lived has a spirit. Your great-great grandparents' spirit is still alive even though their bodies aren't. Your friends all have spirits. People you meet at school have a spirit. You have a spirit.

There's even something unexplainably spiritual about nature. God speaks to us through the way we relate to trees, animals and all of his creation.

Choose to be around positive spirits. You know when someone has a negative spirit. Don't let those spirits get close to yours. Too often, it is the bad spirit that rubs off on the good one, rather than the other way around. Protect your spirit as if it was a golden treasure—because it is.

I am smart, happy and healthy. My parents love me. God has given me many gifts. I can do anything I want to if I make a plan, concentrate and work toward it every day.

# You cannot walk through a closed door.

We spend our lives moving. We move from one place to another. We move from one grade to another. We move from one school to another or from one job to another. Sometimes when we want to make a move, it seems as if all of the doors are closed to us.

If a door is closed, you can stand there and beat on the door.

Or you can look for a door that is open. Or maybe you can use that little thing attached to the door...the doorknob.

As you go through life, you are going to have to look for the way to get from where you are to where you want to be.
It will not always be obvious.

And the door will not always be where you want it to be.

I am smart, happy and healthy. My parents love me. God has given me many gifts. I can do anything I want to if I make a plan, concentrate and work toward it every day.

No matter how old you are, the most important thing you can do today is get better.

# Learn something new.

Read. When you play, play harder and better than you did yesterday.

If you're not getting better, you're probably getting worse. That's not any fun.

I am smart, happy and healthy. My parents love me. God has given me many gifts. I can do anything I want to if I make a plan, concentrate and work toward it every day.

# Love is the most valuable gift

that you can receive—or give.

Before you were even born, your parents loved you. God loved you. You did not do anything to earn that love; it was something they freely gave to you.

As you go through life and meet other people, some of them will love you. You may be able to do things that help people *like* you (or not like you), but you cannot do anything to force a person to love you.

When a person gets to really know you, they will either decide to offer you their love or not.

I am smart, happy and healthy. My parents love me. God has given me many gifts. I can do anything I want to if I make a plan, concentrate and work toward it every day.

# Someone has to win.
### Why shouldn't it be you?

In every contest, there is a winner. Someone has the lead role in every play. Someone has to make the best grades in the class or be the best musician in the band.

Why shouldn't that someone be you? Winners and excellent performers don't happen by accident. They happen because someone chooses to be that way. They make a decision. They make a plan. And they practice. They work for it.

If you want to be the winner, that's how you do it.

I am smart, happy and healthy. My parents love me. God has given me many gifts. I can do anything I want to if I make a plan, concentrate and work toward it every day.

## October 24th

Birthday of Steven Covey
Author of *First Things First*
1932

# Always do the most important things first.

There are lots of things we do in our lives that are fun but aren't as important as some other things. If we do the most important things first, we will enjoy the rest of our day even more.

Do your homework before you play. Then when you play, you won't have to worry about the homework that you still have to do. Make your bed and clean your room first thing in the morning. It is a great way to start your day, doesn't take much time, and it makes it easy to answer "yes" if your parents ask you if you have done your jobs.

Doing the most important things first makes it easier to enjoy the rest of your life.

I am smart, happy and healthy. My parents love me. God has given me many gifts. I can do anything I want to if I make a plan, concentrate and work toward it every day.

There are some things that

# you will never understand.

Don't be upset about it.
Some things in life are a mystery.
What happens after we die? What is God?

How does that rope in the swimming pool keep the
deep water from getting into the shallow end?
Does the light stay on or go off when
you close the refrigerator door?

Obviously some mysteries are more
important and more mysterious than others.

Don't ever give up trying to learn something
simply because it is hard. And don't get
frustrated because it is impossible.

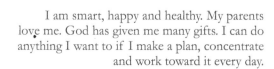

I am smart, happy and healthy. My parents
love me. God has given me many gifts. I can do
anything I want to if I make a plan, concentrate
and work toward it every day.

## October 26th

No matter how good you are,

# you can be better.

The greatest athletes in the world practice their sport every day. Seven days a week they do something to help themselves get better. Why do they do this? Because they know they aren't perfect.

There has never been a perfect writer, musician, football player or actor. Everyone can get better at their passion, even if they are already the best in the world.

I am smart, happy and healthy. My parents love me. God has given me many gifts. I can do anything I want to if I make a plan, concentrate and work toward it every day.

# Always write thank-you notes.

The written word is powerful. When someone goes to the trouble of doing something nice for you, you should do something nice back for them.

A handwritten note is one of the best gifts you can give.

Get into the habit of writing a note to someone every day. Take five minutes to write someone: a grandparent, friend, parent—anyone. Write a note just to say hello.

Then, when someone gives you a gift, you will already be in the habit of writing notes. Writing them a thank-you note will be easy.

I am smart, happy and healthy. My parents love me. God has given me many gifts. I can do anything I want to if I make a plan, concentrate and work toward it every day.

## October 28th

Birthday of Bill Gates
Founder of Microsoft and the Gates Foundation
1955

# The happiest people are givers.

If you study the people who have the most money, some of them are happy; some of them are very sad. What is the difference?

One difference is that the happiest people are the ones who do things for others. They are givers. Some of the saddest people are those who keep their money to themselves, never sharing it with anyone.

This is also true of people who keep their toys to themselves. Or their laughter to themselves. Or their jokes, great ideas or love.

You may not have a lot of money, but you have things you can give to others. If you want to be sad, keep those gifts to yourself. If you want to be happy, share.

I MADE THIS
BOOMERANG
FOR YOU

I am smart, happy and healthy. My parents love me. God has given me many gifts. I can do anything I want to if I make a plan, concentrate and work toward it every day.

# Life is about collecting experiences.

There are a lot of things in life that you can collect. You will become bored with most of them over time... things like dolls, stuffed animals and socks on your bedroom floor. Many of the things people collect become worn out or they get lost.

The best thing in life to collect is a great experience. You can never lose it. It will never wear out.

When you have the chance to do something unique and exciting, or be with someone who will teach you something, take advantage of that opportunity. It might create an experience that you will remember the rest of your life.

I am smart, happy and healthy. My parents love me. God has given me many gifts. I can do anything I want to if I make a plan, concentrate and work toward it every day.

# Every problem

is an opportunity to learn something about yourself.

When things don't go your way, always ask yourself,
"What can I learn from this situation?" Maybe you
made a mistake that caused the problem. If so, admit
it and try to figure out how not to do that again.

Maybe no one made a mistake. Perhaps life simply gave
you a bad situation. If so, how do you deal with it?
If you deal with it successfully, you have learned
how to work on problems.

If you don't do a good job of dealing with the problem,
you have also learned something. You have learned how
not to deal with problems.

Both of these are useful lessons. Always learn
from the problems in your life.

I HAVE
HOW
MUCH
HOMEWORK??

I am smart, happy and healthy. My parents
love me. God has given me many gifts. I can do
anything I want to if I make a plan, concentrate
and work toward it every day.

# A boat with no engine or sail,

just drifting in a river, will crash.

When you are in a boat, you don't need an engine to float. You can just let the water take you wherever it wants to.

Many people are like that in life. They never turn on their engines or use their steering wheels. They just get up each morning, with no plan, and let the river of life take them wherever it wants to. They don't know where they are going and, many times, they end up at places where they wish they weren't.

If you use your motor and steering wheel there is no guarantee you'll go where you want to go. If you don't use them, however, you are guaranteed to get lost or crash.

I am smart, happy and healthy. My parents love me. God has given me many gifts. I can do anything I want to if I make a plan, concentrate and work toward it every day.

# Don't worry about the past.

Learn from it.

When something has happened, it's over. You cannot change it. If you thought you should have made an A on a test but you made a B, you can sit around and mope all day long, but it will not change your grade.

If you and your best friend got into an argument, you can stay mad at her and complain to all of your other friends, but it won't repair your friendship.

This doesn't mean you should ignore the past. Try to figure out what you did to cause the argument between you and your friend. What could you have done differently to make your grade better?

Use the past as a laboratory. It is a place where you experiment to see what does and does not work.

I am smart, happy and healthy. My parents love me. God has given me many gifts. I can do anything I want to if I make a plan, concentrate and work toward it every day.

# Be clear about your goals.

To be happy or successful, you must know what success is. When you can define success, you can set your goals.

When you are clear about your goals, it's easy to decide how to spend your time. You know what's important to you. You know what things you need to learn how to do.

This is the first step toward success.

I am smart, happy and healthy. My parents love me. God has given me many gifts. I can do anything I want to if I make a plan, concentrate and work toward it every day.

# If you don't take care of your responsibilities,

it hurts your parents, but it hurts you more.

If you are supposed to make your bed, take out the trash or just keep the house clean, it makes more work and problems for your parents if you don't.

It really hurts you more than them, though. Every time you do what you are supposed to do, it makes you a little stronger. It makes you ready for a little more responsibility.

It helps you grow up just a little bit.

Every time you don't do your work, though, you are getting less mature. It's like going from being eight years old to being five years old.

If you want to grow up and be able to do more adult things, do what you are supposed to do. And if you want to grow up more quickly, do more than you are supposed to do.

I am smart, happy and healthy. My parents love me. God has given me many gifts. I can do anything I want to if I make a plan, concentrate and work toward it every day.

# Envy is like rust on your soul.

## It slowly eats away at you.

Envy is when you see something that another person has and you are sad because they have it and you don't. "Little Susie has a Super Duper Doozie Doll and I want one. Why can't I have a Super Duper Doozie Doll? I just have to have one."

That is envy.

Have you ever seen rust eat away at a piece of metal that has been scratched and left sitting outside? Rust will completely eat even strong metal.

Envy is the same way. When you envy someone, it eats away at your soul just like rust. It doesn't hurt the other person; it hurts you.

I am smart, happy and healthy. My parents love me. God has given me many gifts. I can do anything I want to if I make a plan, concentrate and work toward it every day.

It doesn't matter whose fault it is,

# make it better.

When something bad happens to you, there are several things you might do. Some people spend their time trying to figure out whose fault it is. Other people don't care whose fault it is, they just start blaming someone else.

The right thing to do, however, is to immediately figure out how to fix the problem or make it better. If it's important, you can worry later about who made the mistake.

The most important thing to do first is fix the problem.

I am smart, happy and healthy. My parents love me. God has given me many gifts. I can do anything I want to if I make a plan, concentrate and work toward it every day.

November 6th

# Your mind is a magnet.

Be careful what you put near it.

If you constantly think about the things that make you afraid, you will increase the chances that those things come into your life.

Don't spend all your energy thinking about what you don't want to happen. Your mind just tries to attract whatever you are thinking about.

You get to decide what you think about, so you can decide what you attract. Spend time thinking about the things you want.

I am smart, happy and healthy. My parents love me. God has given me many gifts. I can do anything I want to if I make a plan, concentrate and work toward it every day.

If you are running down the wrong road,

# quit running.

Sometimes people are very busy in their lives but they aren't moving toward their goal. Maybe they are moving in no particular direction. Or worse, maybe they are moving away from the things that are important to them.

Stop and look at your direction.
If it is not toward your goals, stop!

I am smart, happy and healthy. My parents love me. God has given me many gifts. I can do anything I want to if I make a plan, concentrate and work toward it every day.

# There is a God–and it isn't you.

It's natural to want things to go our way, and there is nothing wrong with that. However, don't get mad when you realize that things don't always go your way. Don't get upset when you finally discover that you can't make people do what you want them to do.

Don't get upset when you are not always the center of everyone's attention.

You do not have this kind of power. You can't control everything. You can't be the center of attention all the time. You have to learn that you are only human, just like the other 6.7 billion people on earth right now.

I am smart, happy and healthy. My parents love me. God has given me many gifts. I can do anything I want to if I make a plan, concentrate and work toward it every day.

*November 9th*

There is a difference
between moving around and

# moving ahead.

Sometimes when we're moving around we're
pretending to solve a problem, but we're just making
things worse—like making muddy water muddier.

There is a difference between trying hard to solve a
problem and simply doing stuff. Sometimes we can find
the answers to our problems if we will stop and listen.

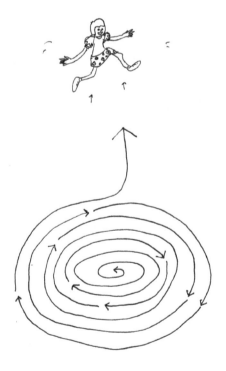

I am smart, happy and healthy. My parents
love me. God has given me many gifts. I can do
anything I want to if I make a plan, concentrate
and work toward it every day.

# What happens in you

is more important than what happens to you.

Every day things happen in your life.
People say nice things to you, or they say mean
things to you. You hope for things; sometimes they
happen and sometimes they don't. Toys will
break. It will rain. The sun will shine.

The most important thing is how you react to
those things. A lot of things happen around you
that you can't control. However, you always
do get to control what you think about.

The things in your brain and in your heart will
affect your life so much more than things
that go on around you.

I am smart, happy and healthy. My parents
love me. God has given me many gifts. I can do
anything I want to if I make a plan, concentrate
and work toward it every day.

The only way to catch a fish is to

# risk losing your worm.

If you drop a fishing line in the water, your hook might get stuck on a log or a fish might take a nibble at it. Lots of things might cause your bait to fall off the hook.

That is a risk you take when you go fishing. Without taking that risk, you would never catch a fish.

Most people don't worry about losing a worm; that's no big deal. But every good thing in life requires some kind of risk. You must be willing to lose or give up something if you want anything good out of life.

Be willing to take risks.

I am smart, happy and healthy. My parents love me. God has given me many gifts. I can do anything I want to if I make a plan, concentrate and work toward it every day.

# Why be average,

when you can be above average?

If you are an average baseball player, it means that you are better than a bunch of other players. It also means that a bunch of players are better than you.

You're not bad. You're not great. You're somewhere in the middle. If you are going to do something, you can choose to do it well. You can practice and work hard. You can ask people to teach you and help you get better.

Someone has to be the best baseball player or the best guitar player or the best speller or the best artist or the best singer or the best gymnast.

It's going to be someone. Why not you?

I am smart, happy and healthy. My parents love me. God has given me many gifts. I can do anything I want to if I make a plan, concentrate and work toward it every day.

*November 13th*

# The longer you hang around a skunk,

the more it begins to smell normal.

Imagine if you played with skunks like you might play with a puppy. The skunks would rub off on you. You would become like a skunk.

You would stink.

If you're around skunks long enough, you wouldn't even notice the stink. Skunks don't.

People are the same way, except usually without the bad smell. You will become like the people you hang around.

Like skunks, if you hang around stinky people long enough, the bad things about that person will seem normal. You won't notice them anymore.

WHAT?

I am smart, happy and healthy. My parents love me. God has given me many gifts. I can do anything I want to if I make a plan, concentrate and work toward it every day.

# Wasting someone else's time is rude.

Your time is valuable. It is more valuable than money.

If your time is more valuable than money, then everyone else's time is more valuable than money, too.

When you tell someone you will be somewhere at a certain time, be there. Don't make them wait for you. If they have to sit around and wait for you, you have wasted their time.

When people depend on you on a team or on a project at school, do what you are supposed to do when you are supposed to do it. If you don't, you are wasting those people's time.

I am smart, happy and healthy. My parents love me. God has given me many gifts. I can do anything I want to if I make a plan, concentrate and work toward it every day.

*November 15th*

# You will never be perfect,

but don't let that stop you from trying.

Everyone makes mistakes. The greatest inventors in the world failed thousands of time before creating things like the light bulb or the airplane. Great writers struggle for years to have their first book published. Presidents and priests make mistakes.

Sometimes even parents do, believe it or not. You are going to make mistakes, too.

There are two ways you can handle this. You can accept the fact that you are going to make mistakes and expect it. Or you can try to be better every day at everything you do. Understand that you will never be *perfect*, but if that is your goal, you will always have a chance to be *better*.

I am smart, happy and healthy. My parents love me. God has given me many gifts. I can do anything I want to if I make a plan, concentrate and work toward it every day.

# Your body and your brain

will always work together.

Have you ever noticed that it's hard to be in a bad mood and smile at the same time? It is confusing. You may feel bad, but your face is trying to act happy. One of them will win. You will either not be able to keep smiling very long or your smile will put you in a good mood.

Your brain is the place where everything about your body starts: your thoughts and every action. Once you have a thought, you set events in motion that have predictable outcomes.

You can't think one thing and do another.

I am smart, happy and healthy. My parents love me. God has given me many gifts. I can do anything I want to if I make a plan, concentrate and work toward it every day.

*November 17th*

When you're doing something tough or hard,

# do it with a happy spirit, even if you have to fake it.

When you are in a great mood, everything is better. You can work better. The people around you are happier, and they can work better, too.

When you are working on something that's hard or difficult, try to be happy while you're doing it. The job will go faster and you will be more likely to do good work.

Besides, if you have a happy spirit while you do it, the job may not be as tough as you first thought.

TONIGHT'S HOMEWORK

I am smart, happy and healthy. My parents love me. God has given me many gifts. I can do anything I want to if I make a plan, concentrate and work toward it every day.

### November 18th

William Tell shot an arrow through an apple sitting
on his son's head
1307

# You cannot hit
# two targets
with one arrow.

If you are going to shoot at a target, you first have to
decide on a target. You can't point an arrow at two or
three different targets and have a chance of hitting
any of them. When you let your arrow fly, you need to
know where you want it to go.

Your energy in life is the same way. If you are
spending your energy in a bunch of different
directions without really knowing what it is you are
trying to do, you probably won't do anything. Your
arrow will fall to the ground without hitting anything.

I am smart, happy and healthy. My parents
love me. God has given me many gifts. I can do
anything I want to if I make a plan, concentrate
and work toward it every day.

# Money isn't good or bad.

It depends on what's in your heart.

Sometimes people will do almost anything to get money. Money, or the things money can buy, becomes the most important thing in their life. Their money or their stuff is more important than their relationships.

This is bad. This is almost like the person is worshipping money.

Other people don't pay any attention to their money. They don't plan. They don't save. They spend money that they shouldn't.

This is bad, too. These people don't care about themselves, or they would plan better.

What you do with money is important, because the way you treat money shows what is in your heart.

I am smart, happy and healthy. My parents love me. God has given me many gifts. I can do anything I want to if I make a plan, concentrate and work toward it every day.

If you're going to use the energy to have dreams, make them good ones.

In many parts of the world, you don't have many decisions about the kinds of things you get to do as an adult. Your parents, schools or maybe even the government make the decisions about what jobs you will have and where you will live as an adult.

People came to America and started a new country so they could do whatever they wanted. We can attend whatever church we want, or none at all. We can live where we want. We can invent new things, create jobs and play games, all because our country is free.

# Dream big.

If you don't, you are wasting a great opportunity.

I am smart, happy and healthy. My parents love me. God has given me many gifts. I can do anything I want to if I make a plan, concentrate and work toward it every day.

# November 21st

The most important type of discipline is
# self-discipline.

As you get just a little older, you begin to make many decisions that your parents used to make for you. Maybe you get to pick your lunch or the clothes you wear. Perhaps you earn money and can decide how to spend it.

Of course, you don't get to make all of your own decisions. You may still have to wake up when your parents tell you to. You don't get to go to the grocery store by yourself. You don't have your own car.

Someday, however, you will be responsible for making all of your own decisions.

You will need discipline to make good decisions when you are an adult—and sometimes no one will be around to help you make those good decisions.

THIS
YUMMY
CAKE
IS FOR
MY MOM

I am smart, happy and healthy. My parents love me. God has given me many gifts. I can do anything I want to if I make a plan, concentrate and work toward it every day.

# The people who make the most mistakes

are the ones who achieve the most.

If you want to achieve a lot of things, you must not be afraid to try things. When you are trying new things, there will be a lot of them that don't work out.

That's okay. The more you try, the more mistakes you will make. But you will also achieve more.

Every time you make a mistake, you learn how *not* to do something. Don't get upset at mistakes; learn from them.

I am smart, happy and healthy. My parents love me. God has given me many gifts. I can do anything I want to if I make a plan, concentrate and work toward it every day.

# You must earn your own respect

before anyone else will respect you.

The only way to respect yourself is to act in a way that is respectable. Be honest. Do what you say you are going to do. Carry out your responsibilities. Treat people like you want to be treated. Treat all of God's creation with respect.

If you do those things, you can respect yourself.

If you don't respect yourself, however, others will be able to tell. And if you know that you are unworthy of respect, no one else will be willing to respect you.

HERE YOU GO, LITTLE GUY!

I am smart, happy and healthy. My parents love me. God has given me many gifts. I can do anything I want to if I make a plan, concentrate and work toward it every day.

# The more you give,

the more you will get.

There are lots of reasons to help other people. When you have been blessed, it is right to share those blessings with people who are less fortunate.

The best way to take care of needy people is one person helping another. This is true whether a person needs food, a place to live or just someone to talk to.

When you help other people, you are making the world a better place. When you make the world better, you are making it better for everyone, including yourself.

I am smart, happy and healthy. My parents love me. God has given me many gifts. I can do anything I want to if I make a plan, concentrate and work toward it every day.

# When you build a fence,

always put a gate in it.

Imagine if a farmer built a fence around his pasture but didn't leave any way to get in and out of the field. It would be hard to be a good farmer, wouldn't it?

He would have to teach his cows or corn to jump over the fence when he was ready to sell them.

Gates make life easier.

When we get mad at people and don't talk to them, we are building different kinds of fences. It is okay to have things that you keep to yourself, but don't ever keep everything to yourself. Keep some gates in your life.

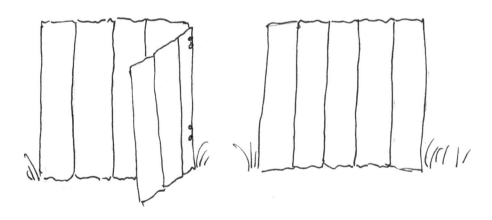

I am smart, happy and healthy. My parents love me. God has given me many gifts. I can do anything I want to if I make a plan, concentrate and work toward it every day.

# Decide what you want.

When you go to a restaurant, a server usually asks what you want to eat. What would happen if you always answered, "I don't know"?

You might not get any food. You sure wouldn't get to decide what food you were going to have. Somebody else would decide.

The only way to have any impact on what you are going to get is to make your own decision. Decide what you want. That's the first step.

That's also the first step in life.

THAT'S IT.

I am smart, happy and healthy. My parents love me. God has given me many gifts. I can do anything I want to if I make a plan, concentrate and work toward it every day.

# Sometimes it's your fault

and you don't even know it.

When something bothers you or you get angry at someone, try to stop and ask yourself this question: What did I do to make this a bad situation?

If you are honest, you will usually realize that the other person isn't the only one to blame: You probably did something wrong also, even if it was just a small wrong.

And if you did anything wrong, you can't be mad at the other person.

I am smart, happy and healthy. My parents love me. God has given me many gifts. I can do anything I want to if I make a plan, concentrate and work toward it every day.

It is easy to become excited about an idea.

# How long will you stay excited?

Success comes to those who remain excited and committed until those ideas are completed.

If you really want to do something, work at it. Work today, tomorrow and the next day. If it is important to you, stay at it as long as it takes, even if it takes months or years.

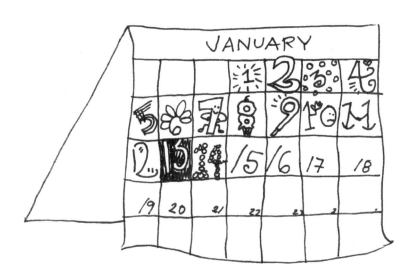

I am smart, happy and healthy. My parents love me. God has given me many gifts. I can do anything I want to if I make a plan, concentrate and work toward it every day.

# Do not make excuses.

With most things in life, you either do them or you don't. Did you complete your homework? That is a yes or no question.

Did you make your bed? Did you put the Jell-O in your sister's shoe? Yes or no?

If there is something you were supposed to do and you didn't do it, don't start making excuses. Just say, "I didn't do that." Don't blame it on someone else. If you put Jell-O in your sister's shoe, don't try to convince your parents that someone else talked you into it.

If you do something wrong, it is your fault. Take responsibility.

I am smart, happy and healthy. My parents love me. God has given me many gifts. I can do anything I want to if I make a plan, concentrate and work toward it every day.

# If you want to know what someone thinks of himself,

listen to him talk about another person.

When we are talking about another person, our words often reflect the way we feel about ourselves at that moment. It is easier to find the good in someone when we feel good about ourselves.

We are also more likely to say bad things about someone when we don't feel good about ourselves.

The same is true of other people. If someone says bad things about you, it says more about the way they feel about themselves than it does about you.

ZACH IS SO SMART. HAVE YOU SEEN HIS SCIENCE PROJECT YET?

I am smart, happy and healthy. My parents love me. God has given me many gifts. I can do anything I want to if I make a plan, concentrate and work toward it every day.

# Pray every day.

There are different ways to pray. As you get older you might try different ways to talk to God and listen to God. That's good.

The important thing is that every day you take some time to thank God for your blessings and ask for the wisdom to make good decisions.

Prayer isn't a year-round wish list of Christmas presents. Prayer is a time when you can be quiet, talk to God, and listen for the wisdom that comes from a power that is greater than you.

I am smart, happy and healthy. My parents love me. God has given me many gifts. I can do anything I want to if I make a plan, concentrate and work toward it every day.

# If you want to be frustrated, ignore the will of God in your life.

Does it ever seem that things always seem to go wrong? Are you having trouble being happy, even though you keep thinking happy thoughts?

If you find yourself in a time like this, look at all the things happening in your life. Are you doing anything in your life that you are ashamed of? Are you treating someone in a way that is mean?

Have you done something wrong to someone and not apologized for it?

Sometimes, but not always, when we find ourselves in a bad place in life, it is because we have done something contrary to the will of God.

DINNERTIME!

UH OH!

I am smart, happy and healthy. My parents love me. God has given me many gifts. I can do anything I want to if I make a plan, concentrate and work toward it every day.

# Dreams are great,

but without action they are worthless.

A lot of people have big dreams and hopes, but they don't do anything about those dreams. Thoughts and plans are great, but you have to take action if you want to achieve anything.

Imagine if you took apple seeds and spread them on hard concrete and never watered them or put the seeds in dirt.

What would happen?

The seeds would die.

So will your dreams if you don't take care of them and work on them every day.

I am smart, happy and healthy. My parents love me. God has given me many gifts. I can do anything I want to if I make a plan, concentrate and work toward it every day.

# We do not find God, we accept him.

Sometimes we try hard to bring God into
our lives. We pray. When things are hard
we might even cry out for help.

There is a goodness and wisdom that
surrounds you—if you will only listen to it.
Maybe it comes to you through another person.
Maybe God speaks to you through your own mind.
Maybe there is some connection that God uses
through nature to provide you with some answers.

We only have to move the clutter out of
our lives and allow the wisdom to come in.

I am smart, happy and healthy. My parents
love me. God has given me many gifts. I can do
anything I want to if I make a plan, concentrate
and work toward it every day.

# December 5th

Birthday of Walt Disney
1901

If you want to be good at anything
or enjoy every day, you must choose to

# have a positive
# mental attitude.

You can't enjoy being at a concert or a carnival or
even being at Walt Disney World if you start off in
a bad mood. Having a positive attitude is necessary
to enjoy anything you are doing.

The great thing is that you get to decide. It's up to you
whether to have a positive attitude or a negative attitude.
Even if everyone around you is in a bad mood, you can
still choose to have a positive mental attitude.

I am smart, happy and healthy. My parents
love me. God has given me many gifts. I can do
anything I want to if I make a plan, concentrate
and work toward it every day.

# Most people complain.
### Don't be one of those people.

Too many people look for the bad things in life. If there are nine happy things going on in their life and only one bad thing, they will complain about the one bad thing. Complaining never helps with anything. It only puts you and all of the people around you in a bad mood.

Some people rarely complain. These people focus on the good things. They are also the people who help make those around them happier.

I am smart, happy and healthy. My parents love me. God has given me many gifts. I can do anything I want to if I make a plan, concentrate and work toward it every day.

*December 7th*

# Practice being polite,

just like you practice anything else.

You have to practice anything if you want to be good at it. Spelling, music, gymnastics, golf—all of these require practice.

Being polite is the same way. Practice it whenever you can. Think about it. What can you do nice for someone right now? Open a door for them? Say "please," "sir" or "ma'am"? The more you think about it, the easier it will be for you to do.

I am smart, happy and healthy. My parents love me. God has given me many gifts. I can do anything I want to if I make a plan, concentrate and work toward it every day.

# Don't regret the past;

don't worry about the future. Enjoy today.

The only thing we have for certain is now. Today. This very moment. Make the most and best of it.

There is nothing you can do to change the past. It's over. Learn from it and go on.

You should plan for the future, but don't plan on it. The future may never come. Tomorrow isn't promised to us.

You know that you have the present. You are in it at this very moment. What are you doing to take advantage of it? Don't waste it. It is precious.

I am smart, happy and healthy. My parents love me. God has given me many gifts. I can do anything I want to if I make a plan, concentrate and work toward it every day.

# If you stop
every time things begin to hurt,
# you will never
# get better.

Our bodies send us pain signals for various reasons, but all pain signals are not the same.

Most of the pain in our life isn't serious. It's like a cut finger or a broken arm. It's just a hurdle.

Hurdles make it harder to get to a goal. They are one of the ways that life separates winners from losers. If there were no pain involved in trying to achieve goals, everyone would be successful.

Most people, however, quit the first or second time things get tough for them. When you are tired or hurting and you continue to push yourself, that's when you are separating yourself from everyone else.

I am smart, happy and healthy. My parents love me. God has given me many gifts. I can do anything I want to if I make a plan, concentrate and work toward it every day.

Every great invention or act first

# began as a thought

someone conceived in their mind.

Before you can achieve your goals in life, you must first know what they are. Before you can invent something or get somewhere, you must know what it is you are trying to do or where you are trying to go.

Your mind is the beginning point for every trip you take, whether it is an actual trip, like a vacation, or a trip of experience, like trying to do something new. Decide what you want. This is the first step to success.

I am smart, happy and healthy. My parents love me. God has given me many gifts. I can do anything I want to if I make a plan, concentrate and work toward it every day.

# Don't take all the credit. Give credit to others.

When you are on a team and something good happens, be sure to tell your teammates what a good job they did. This is true on a sports team, at home, on a school project or if something good happens at your job.

When you give other people the credit, it makes them feel good about themselves. They will want to work hard and smart the next time they are on a team with you.

If you take the credit, few people, if anyone, will want to work with you again.

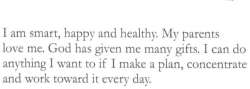

I am smart, happy and healthy. My parents love me. God has given me many gifts. I can do anything I want to if I make a plan, concentrate and work toward it every day.

# Look for the best in people.

When you first meet someone, there are two things you can do. You could start looking for the things you think are wrong with them. Maybe they talk funny or you don't like their hair.

The other thing you could do is to start looking for good things about the other person. Have they lived somewhere interesting? Do they play a musical instrument or sport that you like? Do they just need a friend?

When you look for the good in someone, it helps people see the good in you. When you are always looking for the bad in others, it makes you look bad, too.

ISN'T SHE BEAUTIFUL?

I am smart, happy and healthy. My parents love me. God has given me many gifts. I can do anything I want to if I make a plan, concentrate and work toward it every day.

# Think about your goals and plans every day.

It's not enough simply to have a goal and be confident that you can achieve it. You must think about your plan and your goals regularly. Think about them in the morning. Review them in the evening. Did you do anything today to move you closer to the things in life that are important to you?

Unless you are regularly thinking about your goals, it's easy to lose sight of those things that you have decided are important to you.

I KNOW I CAN,
I KNOW I CAN!

I am smart, happy and healthy. My parents love me. God has given me many gifts. I can do anything I want to if I make a plan, concentrate and work toward it every day.

# Everyone needs a purpose.

A purpose is the main thing you are working toward in life. It is the thing that is most important to you.

Your purpose when you are seven years old is different than when you are 17 or 27 years old. Your goals are different.

When you are in elementary school, your major purpose is learning. You should love school and everything about learning. This includes learning about people, about yourself and how to learn. You are learning how to love and how to help others.

As you get older, your purpose will change. If you are going to be a complete person, you must have a purpose. Without it, you will never be as happy as you should be.

I am smart, happy and healthy. My parents love me. God has given me many gifts. I can do anything I want to if I make a plan, concentrate and work toward it every day.

# Don't be disappointed
by little problems.

When something doesn't go your way, it's easy
to get upset and frustrated. Maybe you become
disappointed about it.

Before you get too upset, ask yourself if this is really a
big deal or not?

Don't put all disappointments in the same category.
Not getting what you want for dinner isn't nearly as
important as making a bad grade on a test. Making a
bad grade on a test isn't as big a deal as having a pet die.

And losing a pet doesn't compare to losing
a member of your family. Not all disappointments are
the same. Treat them differently.

I am smart, happy and healthy. My parents
love me. God has given me many gifts. I can do
anything I want to if I make a plan, concentrate
and work toward it every day.

# We are what we do

when no one is watching.

Character is not a show that we put on for someone else.
Character is what we believe about our relationships
with other people and everything around us.
Will we treat others well? Will we treat the earth with respect?

Will we do these things all the time,
or just when we think someone is watching?

I am smart, happy and healthy. My parents
love me. God has given me many gifts. I can do
anything I want to if I make a plan, concentrate
and work toward it every day.

# When you are honest

it does something healthy for your soul.

Your soul is a living thing that is always becoming either more or less healthy. When we do bad things, our soul gets a little sick.

That's like saying we move a little away from God. Every time we do something good, we make our soul a little stronger. We bring ourselves a little closer to God.

We become prepared to face whatever challenge might happen next in our lives. It makes us ready to achieve our goals.

I am smart, happy and healthy. My parents love me. God has given me many gifts. I can do anything I want to if I make a plan, concentrate and work toward it every day.

# If two people are together long enough, they will disagree about things.

There is nothing wrong with that.

It is okay to tell someone—even a parent—your opinion.

You should always do this in a respectful way, especially when the other person is your parent or anyone older than you.

Do not raise your voice. Do not call the other person names. Do not tell the other person that they are wrong, even if they are. Instead, tell them your opinion.

"I think that we should have ice cream for dinner" is a much better statement than, "Broccoli is a stupid food. You are an idiot to eat broccoli."

BEING A MASCOT IS BETTER THAN PLAYING.

I am smart, happy and healthy. My parents love me. God has given me many gifts. I can do anything I want to if I make a plan, concentrate and work toward it every day.

# December 19th

When you go to bed tonight, what's the one thing you will look back and wish you had done today? Do it.

There are lots of things you can save in life. Money. Aluminum cans. Cow bones. Books. But you can't save time. Once a minute or hour or day has passed, it is gone forever. You can never get it back. That's why it is important to make every minute count.

Don't have any regrets today. If there is something important that you want or need to do, do it! Don't go to bed tonight thinking "I wish that today I had...BLANK."

# No excuses. No regrets.

I am smart, happy and healthy. My parents love me. God has given me many gifts. I can do anything I want to if I make a plan, concentrate and work toward it every day.

If you want to change something in your life,

# first change your thoughts.

All change begins in your mind. Before you can do something, you must first decide to do it. If you are sitting in a chair and then walk across the room, you must first decide to get out of the chair. Your legs do not lift you up by themselves.

If you are making a B in spelling at school, you will not make an A until you decide to do better. It will not happen accidentally. You will have to study more and make the decision to make better grades.

All things are this way. Change begins in your mind.

I am smart, happy and healthy. My parents love me. God has given me many gifts. I can do anything I want to if I make a plan, concentrate and work toward it every day.

*December 21st*

Sometimes when something bad happens, you might want to blame the person who delivers the bad news or the person who tries to correct you. That's pretty silly.

If you make a mistake, then the problem is with you. Don't get mad at the other person.

# It's your fault when you mess up.

BETHANY, WHERE'S YOUR HOMEWORK?

I am smart, happy and healthy. My parents love me. God has given me many gifts. I can do anything I want to if I make a plan, concentrate and work toward it every day.

# It is better to fess up

than cover up.

No matter how hard you try, sometimes things are going to happen that you wish didn't happen. Maybe you accidentally break something. You might do something to hurt somebody.

There will even be times in your life that you say something that you shouldn't say. No one wants to tell a lie, but sometimes we do.

When you make a mistake, admit it.

Admit it right away. Don't wait. Don't make another mistake or tell another lie by trying to keep someone from finding out. It may hurt to tell the truth, but it is always much worse to try to hide the truth.

I am smart, happy and healthy. My parents love me. God has given me many gifts. I can do anything I want to if I make a plan, concentrate and work toward it every day.

## December 23rd

# Enjoy the wait.

There are many things in life that we wish would hurry up and happen. Most times, there is little that we can do to speed the process. Things take as long as they take.

You can't make school get out any quicker and you can't make your birthday come any sooner.

And Christmas isn't going to come until December 25, no matter how much you wish it would hurry.

So when you have to wait, enjoy it. Try to quit thinking about tomorrow, and do something with someone to enjoy today. Call someone you haven't talked to in a while. Make someone a present. Spend some extra time praying or alone in nature.

Enjoy today. Don't "wish it away."

I am smart, happy and healthy. My parents love me. God has given me many gifts. I can do anything I want to if I make a plan, concentrate and work toward it every day.

## *December 24th*

Birthday of Howard Hughes
Builder of the largest airplane ever
to fly and once the world's richest man
1905

If you can change your attitude,

# you can change your direction.

Your mental attitude is the way you think about things. Are you happy? Or are you sad? That is your mental attitude.

Your mental attitude is like the wings on a giant airplane. If you can tilt the wings a little bit, you will change where the airplane is headed. Once you change the wings and point the airplane in the direction you want it to go, it is much easier to stay on path.

First, you have to tilt the wings. Change the attitude and the results will follow.

I am smart, happy and healthy. My parents love me. God has given me many gifts. I can do anything I want to if I make a plan, concentrate and work toward it every day.

# December 25th

Christmas Day

Christmas is not just a day on a calendar;
it is a feeling in your heart.

Once a year, a big fat guy in a funny red suit sneaks
into your house, eats cookies and leaves toys.
That's one type of Christmas.

Another Christmas story is about the birth of a baby. His
family was poor, they didn't have a fancy house or fancy
friends, but this is the type of person God chose to show
himself through.

What does this mean? If God was in that poor young
Mother Mary and her little baby lying in a pile of straw,
then

# God is in all of us—every day.

We just have to stop, listen and feel his presence.
And we can do that every day of the year.

I am smart, happy and healthy. My parents
love me. God has given me many gifts. I can do
anything I want to if I make a plan, concentrate
and work toward it every day.

The best way to be happy is to
# help someone else.

We often think that we will be happy if we get certain things. Maybe you think you would be happy if your brother or sister would quit pestering you. Or if you had a pony or a new video game, that might make you happy.

But once we have some pretty basic needs taken care of in our life, getting things won't really make us feel better.

To feel best about ourselves, we should help another person. It's hard to explain, but when we help another person, we also help ourselves. We make ourselves stronger. We remind ourselves that we are part of something bigger than just one person or one small thing.

It also reminds us that sometimes we need help and should be willing to accept it gladly.

I am smart, happy and healthy. My parents love me. God has given me many gifts. I can do anything I want to if I make a plan, concentrate and work toward it every day.

# You only get one body. Take care of it.

What if you had one pair of shoes and you knew
you would never get another pair? You would take
care of those shoes, wouldn't you? You
certainly wouldn't lose them.

God gave you only one body. You have one heart,
one set of lungs, one group of muscles. You have
to make this body last your entire life.

This is the only body you get.

Every time you do something bad to your body, you are
doing a little damage that you may not ever be able to
fix. Every little good thing adds up, too. When you eat
the right foods, exercise, get good sleep, work hard and
keep your body clean, you are taking care of the place
you have to live your whole life: in your body.

I am smart, happy and healthy. My parents
love me. God has given me many gifts. I can do
anything I want to if I make a plan, concentrate
and work toward it every day.

# Dreams are inspirations

we give ourselves.

Nothing is ever achieved without a dream. Dreams push you to the top and allow you to be the person that you want to be.

Even if your dream sounds crazy, don't let people crush your dreams. Keep pushing until you achieve what you want.

You may fall short of your dreams, but that is okay. You also learn by your mistakes. If you give up when you hit a bump in the road, you will never accomplish your dream.

I am smart, happy and healthy. My parents love me. God has given me many gifts. I can do anything I want to if I make a plan, concentrate and work toward it every day.

*December 29th*

Most real problems are like a balloon stuck on an air hose; the longer you wait, the bigger they get. And if you wait long enough, they eventually blow up.

When something happens in your life that you think is a problem, the first thing to do is figure out whether you can actually do anything about it or not. If there's nothing you can do to help or fix the situation, quit worrying about it.

If you can fix the situation, however, do it right away. Don't wait. The best time to fix a problem is as soon as you find it.

# Deal with your problems; don't avoid them.

I am smart, happy and healthy. My parents love me. God has given me many gifts. I can do anything I want to if I make a plan, concentrate and work toward it every day.

# Work harder.

Some people might be smarter than you. Others might be taller or have more hair or have more teeth.

You can't do anything about those things.

You can control how hard you work. You are the only person who decides that.

At different times in your life, you will be competing with someone who has an advantage over you that you can't do anything about. He or she might have three or four advantages over you.

But if you set your mind to it, you can outwork anyone. In fact, you can outwork everyone. That's more important than almost anything.

I am smart, happy and healthy. My parents love me. God has given me many gifts. I can do anything I want to if I make a plan, concentrate and work toward it every day.

# How are you doing toward your goals?

Are there any changes you should make to help you achieve your goals? You need to measure how you're doing to know if you need to make any changes or not.

And if you need to make any changes, start today—not tomorrow.

If your goals still seem right, and you're working your plan to reach them, take a moment to feel good about yourself.

I am smart, happy and healthy. My parents love me. God has given me many gifts. I can do anything I want to if I make a plan, concentrate and work toward it every day.